Take It Personal

Take It Personal

How to Succeed by Building Relationships and Playing the Long Game

David Grutman

Foreword by Kim Kardashian

zando

NEW YORK

zandoprojects.com

First Edition: April 2026

Text design by Kevin Ullrich
Cover design by LoveFrom

The publisher does not have control over and is not responsible for author
or other third-party websites (or their content).

Library of Congress Control Number: 2025948062

978-1-63893-349-6 (Hardcover)
978-1-63893-350-2 (ebook)

10 9 8 7 6 5 4 3 2
Manufactured in the United States of America
LBK

I dedicate this book to my wonderful wife, Isabela; our two children, Kaia and Vida; and to all those who taught me to take it personal.

Contents

Take It Personal

FOREWORD

When I think about David Grutman, the first words that come to mind are *energy, vision,* and *loyalty.* From the moment you meet him, you feel the force of his presence: He's someone who not only walks into a room but transforms it. Over the years, I've had the privilege of watching David turn ideas into iconic destinations and friendships into lifelong bonds.

David isn't just a hospitality king; he's a builder of experiences. Whether it's creating a space where people feel alive, curating unforgettable moments, or cultivating genuine connections, he has mastered the art of bringing people together. And trust me, in a world where trends come and go faster than ever, that kind of staying power comes only from real heart, discipline, and an unmatched ability to see opportunity where others don't.

But what I admire most about David, and what makes this book so special, is that he's willing to share the lessons behind the glamour. The setbacks, the pivots, the moments when things could have gone either way—David embraces them all as part of his story. He reminds us that success isn't about avoiding mistakes but about learning from them and using them to fuel what comes next.

As a friend, I've seen firsthand how deeply he cares about the people around him. His generosity, humor, and authenticity are constants, no matter how big the stage gets. Reading these pages, you'll feel that same connection. It's David inviting you into his world, not just the bright lights and champagne toasts but the wisdom that comes from building something lasting.

So, as you open this book, get ready to laugh, be inspired, and maybe even rethink the way you approach your own dreams. David has lived these lessons, and now he's passing them on. And if there's one thing I know about my friend, it's this: When David Grutman has something to teach, you definitely want to listen.

I remember the very first time I met David. It was in Miami, which makes sense, because Miami *is* David. The city has this pulse—it's vibrant, colorful, alive at all hours—and David embodies all of that. People sometimes underestimate how much environment influences who we become, but in David's case, it's like the city and the man are reflections of each other.

David's influence started in Miami, but what he built is a masterclass in market diversification. He created an ecosystem—a flywheel where a VIP experience at LIV drives traffic to Komodo, which drives buzz for his hotels, and so on. That's not just hospitality; that's strategic scaling. As a businesswoman focused on high-growth ventures, I recognize that kind of synergy. David doesn't just chase trends; he engineers a self-sustaining culture, and that's a billion-dollar lesson in business.

I think about all the times I've been in one of David's spaces, surrounded by people from all over the world. That's when it hits you—he's created places where cultures blend, where barriers drop, where people who might never cross paths end up sharing a moment they'll never forget. That's powerful. That's legacy.

What struck me immediately wasn't just his confidence but his openness. He has this way of making you feel like you've known him forever, even if you've just been introduced. That's not a trait you come across often, especially in industries where people are always "on." With David, it's never a performance—it's real. He genuinely wants to know you, to understand you, and to make sure that when you're in his world, you feel seen and celebrated.

And I felt that. I've felt it every time since. Whether at LIV or a quiet dinner with friends, David has a way of turning any gathering into a night to remember.

David's career is proof of what happens when vision meets relentless work. Opening a nightclub might sound glamorous—and in many ways it is—but what people don't always see is the risk, the sleepless nights, the constant need to adapt. David saw possibilities where others saw roadblocks. He didn't just want to create venues; he wanted to create experiences.

Think about LIV. It's not just a club—it's a pop-culture icon all its own. People come from all over the world because they know it's the place to be. That doesn't just happen by chance. It takes foresight, intuition, and yes, a little bit of magic.

But the truth is, David has never been about one project. Every new restaurant, every new venue, every collaboration is an extension of his belief that people need spaces where they can connect.

We live in a time when so much of our interaction happens on our phones, but David reminds us that nothing replaces the feeling of being in a room, dancing with strangers who become friends, sharing a meal that turns into a memory.

David doesn't hide the hard parts. He'll tell you about the moments when he didn't know if something would work or when doors closed before he could even knock. That's rare. So often, success is presented as a straight line: You dream, you work, you achieve. But anyone who's lived it knows that's never the case.

David is proof that resilience is as important as vision. He's faced setbacks and used them as fuel. He's been told no and turned it into yes. And through it all, he's stayed true to himself and to the people he loves. That balance—of being ambitious without losing authenticity—is something I really admire.

Beyond the career, beyond the nightlife, beyond the restaurants— there's David, the friend. His big smile is infectious, and being around him is a lesson in what it's like to know someone is really in your corner.

If you're lucky enough to call David a friend, you know what I mean. He shows up. He celebrates your wins as if they were his own. He's there when things don't go as planned. He'll make you laugh when you need it most, and he'll remind you of your own strength when you've forgotten it.

I've seen him do this not just for me, but for so many people. He creates community everywhere he goes, and that's rare. In a world where it's easy to get caught up in yourself, David never loses sight of the people around him. He thrives on connection, and he gives more than he takes.

Friendships always teach us something, and David has taught me so much. He's taught me the value of showing up with full energy. He's taught me the power of dreaming big but also the importance of doing the work to back it up. He's taught me that generosity isn't about what you give but how you make people feel.

And maybe most importantly, he's taught me that success isn't just about reaching the top—it's about bringing people with you. David never shines alone; he shines with his community, his family, his friends. That's what makes his story so inspiring.

So, as you read this book, I hope you feel what I feel when I think about David. The energy. The vision. The loyalty. But also the lessons, the wisdom, and the pep talks we all need from time to time.

This isn't just the story of a man who built a hospitality empire. It's the story of someone who understands that life is richer when it's shared.

So laugh. Be inspired. Rethink your dreams. And let David's journey remind you that anything is possible when you believe in yourself and in the people around you.

Kim Kardashian

INTRODUCTION

People have called me a lot of things over the years—"the key holder of Miami," an entrepreneur, a connector, a creator, a guy who knows everyone. But none of those labels ever told the whole story. What I really am, and what I've always been, is someone who takes it personal.

Those three words—take it personal—are the words I live by.

When I look back at my career—the late nights, the early mornings, and the days where I was working both late at night *and* early in the morning—it's clear that nothing came easy. Every club and restaurant I've opened, every brand I've invested in, every chance I've taken was built on sleepless nights, unselfish acts, and an obsession with getting things right. I didn't get here by following a nine-to-five playbook. I got here because I was willing to wake up at 8:00 a.m. and still be working at 5:00 a.m. the next day, to ensure every person who walked through my doors felt something.

There's a certain kind of fire you need to keep going when most people would stop. It's the thing inside you that doesn't let you quit, even when everything around you says you should. It's what pushes you through when logic, money, and convenience all tell you to slow down. That fire has carried me through the best and worst moments of my life.

Taking it personal isn't about ego. It's about ownership. It's about caring so deeply that you can't help but give more than you should. It's about refusing to coast. It's the belief that if your name is attached to something—an idea, a place, a person—you owe it your full self. And that kind of passion, that refusal to be casual about your work or your relationships, is the difference between good and unforgettable.

You'll often hear people in business say, "Don't take it so personal." But that never sat right with me. It felt like they were telling me not to care. If something matters to you, if it's worth your time, how can you *not* take it personal? I've never been able to separate who I am from what I do. When I build something, I build it with my name, my time, my energy, and my heart. When I connect with people, I connect from the core. When I make a promise, I mean it. I take it all personally—because that's the only way I know how to give it everything I've got.

When I look back on my career to this point, the throughline is relationships. The connections I've built—personally and professionally— are so precious to me, and when people ask me for guidance or advice, relationships are always what I return to. I believe in myself and my ability to be a leader, but I know that how I got those skills goes back to the relationships I've built and my ability to add value wherever I can.

I believe in getting to know everyone, not just the people you think are most important. Imagine you're at a dinner, and there's someone huge at the table. A power player in your industry. A star. Someone you're trying to close a deal with. It's tempting to focus only on them, to home in and ignore the rest of the table. But that's a mistake. You should talk to every single person at that table. You've got to be present with everyone because people notice that stuff. They notice when you treat someone like they matter, and they definitely notice when you don't. Artists and musicians and designers and investors come to Miami all the time, and I'll take them and their friends to dinner. In those instances, I always make certain to focus on the other people at the table as well. For one, celebrities don't always want to be fawned over or feel like they're sitting with fans; it's a lot of pressure. They're typically more comfortable when you're comfortable and the vibe is casual. It also puts you in a position to get to know everyone and hear their stories. I've had interactions like this turn into amazing deals down the line, but I've also had plenty of conversations that were just . . . good conversations, and I'm thrilled about that. I love storytelling, and I love hearing the stories other people have to tell. People can tell when you're always on the make, and slowing down and taking the time to really get to know someone else—even if it's just five minutes!—is a great way to show the world that you're someone who values other people. I've learned to not only listen when someone is speaking to me but also to ask follow-up questions and learn. It's not always about how rich or famous someone is or what they can do for you—I'd argue that it should never be about that. Often, it's an unexpected person who will bring something to the table or offer you some kind of knowledge that will help you in the future.

When it comes to business—and to life—I believe the best thing you can do is play the long game. Most of the time, good things will come back to you ten times over, sometimes in ways you'd never expect.

These achievements haven't come to me through sheer luck, and they certainly haven't come without obstacles along the way. Once upon a time, I was a smart-ass kid getting kicked out of prep school, and when I graduated from college, my grand plan was to spend six months tending bar before I grew up and got a "real" job. Even later, after I'd managed and opened successful nightlife venues and restaurants all over Miami, I didn't know how much was still ahead of me in business and in life. I've built a company, sold a company, bought *back* the company, and, in 2019, sold a 51 percent stake in my business to Live Nation.

When I first founded Groot Hospitality, I had no expectation that it would explode into the massive portfolio I operate today. In the Miami area alone, Groot Hospitality owns five restaurants (and counting!) including Gekkō (in partnership with Bad Bunny), Casadonna (in partnership with Tao Group Hospitality), Komodo, and Papi Steak (with David "Papi" Einhorn). We've expanded both our restaurant and nightclub portfolios, including LIV, to Las Vegas and Dallas, while investing in businesses and brands, and pursuing opportunities to bring my signature brand of hospitality around the world.

People see my success, and their first question is always: How did you do it?

The answer is incredibly simple, but in no way easy: I saw opportunities and ran with them. I reestablished the Miami area as a modern hotspot by envisioning dining, hospitality, and nightlife through a lens of lavish design, in-demand talent, a frisson of celebrity, social media moments, and, most importantly, fun that people will remember for the rest of their lives. As time went on, I began to recognize the global appeal of this formula, and I'm constantly looking for ways to expand and refine my ecosystem. I'm also a husband to my beautiful, brilliant wife, Isabela, and our incredible daughters, Kaia and Vida, and I've had to learn lessons there, too: how to balance work and family, how to build relationships that feel like home no matter where in the world we are, and how to be present with the ones I love the most.

I get into it all in "The David Grutman Experience," the entrepreneurship course I teach at Florida International University. I walk students through what it takes to conceptualize and create a leading hospitality platform. In 2023, we had 450 students in the class. Each week focuses on a different topic in the world of entrepreneurship and hospitality, and I also bring in guests who I think students can learn from; they've included David and Victoria Beckham, Jason Momoa, Drake, Kendall Jenner, Hailey Bieber, and Serena Williams, to name a few. We cover their journeys, their mistakes, and the relationships that sit at the foundation of every business empire. I talk about the highs of my career and about the lows and when, early on, I made mistakes I still think about. But I also talk about what I've learned from those mistakes. I've learned when to trust my intuition and when to ask for advice or feedback from the people I've built long-term relationships with based on trust, respect, and honesty.

I've been in the hospitality business for thirty years. I've opened clubs and restaurants that get global attention, and I've worked with people who are the best in the world at what they do. There is a special sense of excitement and nerves, different from a venue opening or a star-studded party. Facing that next generation and trying to get them excited about this industry is something I take personal.

In that classroom, there are no smoke and mirrors. It's just me, standing there, being real. I'm talking about how to dream bigger, how to work harder, how to bounce back from failure and stay hungry for success. During each class, I make sure to build in plenty of time for Q+As, and I encourage students to dig deep and really ask me anything they want to know. Over the course of my career, I've seen a lot of success and I've seen a lot of mistakes—I've also faced plenty of my own challenges. If a lesson I've learned the hard way can help someone just starting out get to where they're trying to go, I want to share it. I don't want to stand up on the classroom's stage blathering about how great I am—I want to be real.

And maybe that's why people connect to my story. Because it's relatable. Everyone wants to see someone they look up to be human, to be vulnerable. And that moment—that classroom, those students—that's the most human I get. And if I can help even one student believe that they can go out and create something amazing, then all the nerves, all the pressure are worth it. I give them the highs and the lows, just as I've seen it unfold in my own career.

When I teach my class, I'm working off a playbook I had to write myself. I've been working in hospitality since the late '90s, and when I started, there weren't any classes like mine. Everything I learned I learned by doing. That's why all the lessons I teach my students—and all the lessons in this book—come from personal experience. I've had incredible successes (which we'll talk about), and I've also had moments that challenged me in ways I could never have imagined. Everything I've seen, done, and experienced has led me to create my own set of guiding principles, centered around respect, honesty, and hard work. Now, with years of teaching my class and decades of business under my belt, I'm ready to put them down on paper.

I really believe in my fundamental principles, and I want to share them with people determined to chase their dreams, achieve success in business and life, and discover the joys of playing the long game. I believe in relationships, and I believe in being honest, thoughtful, and trustworthy. I've made and owned mistakes, I've learned how to parlay one successful venture into another, and I've thought about what kind of legacy I want to leave behind. I think—actually, I know—playing the long game and investing in yourself and your relationships will pay dividends for the rest of your career. Launching a brand is one thing, but building a legacy brand that stands the test of time is another. I'm excited to share my own adventures—and misadventures—in hospitality, entrepreneurship, and brand-building.

If there's one thing I can say for sure, it's that my journey hasn't been lackluster. It's been unpredictable, exhilarating, and emotionally and physically demanding. And I've loved every minute of it.

You have to make your own opportunities in life and be comfortable taking risks. If you can't bet on yourself, who can you bet on?

And with that: Let the journey begin.

CHAPTER ONE

THROWING IT BACK

Naples, Florida, is two-and-a-half hours from Miami, but it might as well be a different planet. It's a beach city, but it draws a totally different crowd. The vibe is more golf carts and early-bird specials than bottle service. I was born there in 1974, and I've been a Florida guy my whole life.

My parents got divorced when I was six, and after that, things shifted for me. My mom was a Realtor, and she worked a lot—especially after hours, since real estate is a 24/7 kind of job—so I have a lot of memories of being home alone. People cared about that kind of thing a lot less in the '80s—I certainly spent more time on my own than my kids ever have. That kind of independence was second nature to me, and I won't lie—I spent a lot of time watching TV. *Charles in Charge, Growing Pains*—all these classic shows about close, tight-knit families were the constant in my life. Looking back, I guess that shaped a lot of who I was—I'd come home from school by myself, do my homework by myself, and get myself fed. I call it being a "stovetop kid"—I was my own short-order cook. When

I got a little older and more social, I'd start working the phones, calling my friends. I'd figure out where to go, how to fill in the gaps of the evening—my first foray into curating nightlife, I guess you could say. Sometimes my mom would take me to work events with her, and she and all her work friends would be amazed at how naturally I jumped into adult conversations—an eleven-year-old kid who could opine on the news of the day was always a hit.

My dad got remarried and had another kid, and I'd see him maybe every couple weeks or so, but it never really felt like family, which is probably why it's so important to me to have a tight-knit family today. It sometimes felt like the three of them were a family unit, and I was on the outside, not quite sure where I fit in. I never really struggled with making friends, but I felt similarly out of place at school. I've had ADHD for as long as I can remember, and while I like to think of myself as a pretty smart guy, when I was a kid, I didn't know how to harness my own attention span. The way we approach kids who think and act differently has changed so much in the last forty years, but in the '80s, it just felt like I could never sit still. I still struggle with it, though at least now I make my own schedule and I don't have to make it through geometry class five days a week.

Eventually, I went to boarding school—a place called Darlington, in Rome, Georgia. It's got that classic prep-school look: brick buildings all covered in ivy. Alumni include politicians, artists, and professional athletes you've definitely heard of. For me . . . let's just say it was a whole other chapter that we don't have time to get into and that I made it all the way to my senior year before getting kicked out for dropping a firecracker down a toilet. Not my brightest moment, but it was in character for where I was at the time. Restless. Testing boundaries. Getting a feel for where I stood in the world.

After that, I ended up at the University of Florida. It was a natural choice for a Florida kid, and I still have close friends and business associates I met while I was there. I graduated in '96, just before the turn of the century—the last of the analog kids stepping into a digital world. I spent four years in Gainesville, and after graduation, I headed back down south, this time to Miami.

At the time, here was my plan:

Get a job tending bar, which I figured I'd do for a year or so, until I'd gotten it out of my system.

Move back to Naples.

Get into title insurance.

Yes, the plan only had three steps, but I figured the rest of my life would sort itself out from there. At the time, the one thing I knew for certain was that I wasn't ready to go back to Naples—not yet.

When I started bartending, I didn't think hospitality could be a career—I didn't even know that hospitality really *was* a career other than a way to make money and have fun while you waited for the rest of your life to start. For me, it was more about the social side. Bartending seemed like a cool thing to do. I'd seen the movie *Cocktail*, watched bartenders in college, watched the way they carried themselves, the energy around them. I was drawn to it.

My initial idea was to get a job bartending somewhere sexy in South Beach, but I quickly learned that the vibe there was more "model slash bartender," heavy emphasis on the model. Hot clubs you had to line up to get into were not trying to hire a chubby twenty-two-year-old Jewish kid to shake up sour apple martinis. So I found myself working at this restaurant in an upscale shopping center in the Biscayne area.

I thought, okay, I'll do this for a year, maybe two, max. My father was the president of SunTrust Bank at the time, and I figured my life would look a lot like his. The world of Naples and office jobs and nice houses in the suburbs was waiting for me. It probably would have been a good life, honestly—but I was meant for something different.

About four or five months into bartending, I felt something change. It was like, for the first time in my life, something clicked. I realized I liked being part of the engine that made everything work. I liked the pressure, the adrenaline, the rhythm of it all. I liked when the bar was slow and I could get to know regulars and memorize their drink orders, and I liked when the bar was packed and I was in the weeds muddling mint for mojitos as fast as humanly possible. The restaurant was in the Aventura Mall, and the mall's owner, Donald Soffer, would come in after playing golf. I'd mix his signature cocktail and we'd chat about life and about the business, and he'd always tip handsomely.

There was a moment where I thought, maybe I don't want to go back. Maybe this is the world I want to be in. Maybe this is the world I want to build in.

As soon as I considered hospitality as a career, I knew I needed to transition from being a bartender to being a manager. I had to start positioning myself as a leader—I had to start *seeing* myself as a leader. It's funny, because the manager works harder and usually makes less money than the bartender. That's just the truth of the industry, and it was true for me. As a bartender, I was clearing $100,000 a year, and my new salary as a manager was $33,000. I quickly found myself working longer hours and feeling more stress, all for a salary that some of the *actual* bartenders probably would have laughed at if they knew. But taking that pay cut was an investment in myself and in my future. I always tell my students: Everything works out in the end! And it did—I bet on myself and never looked back.

Becoming a manager—becoming a leader—meant it was now my responsibility to think about every aspect of hospitality. The atmosphere. The idea that you could shape an entire night, an entire experience, just by how you managed the floor or how you ran the bar. When I was the bartender, I showed up when the schedule told me to. Now, I was the one making the schedule. When people on the team looked to a leader for answers, it was me they were looking to.

And from there, things just kept evolving. I found myself moving up in that world. I started to learn the ropes—inventory, scheduling, people management, all of it. I started to understand that hospitality, when it's done right, is an art form. It's not just serving drinks or food. It's creating a space where people feel something. Where they connect with each other and with you and your business. In any given city, there are a thousand options when it comes to drinks, dinner, and dancing, and I learned very early on never to take it for granted that someone wanted to spend their money and their time in one of my places. I'd touch tables and see first dates, engagements, bachelorette parties, wedding anniversaries—all these special moments that, for these guests, would now forever be linked to the atmosphere I was working so hard to create.

That's what kept me in it. That sense of connection. That, and the fact that I didn't want to go back to that small-town version of my life, that safe, predictable version of myself waiting in Naples. I think some part of me always felt like I had to prove something—to myself, mostly. That I could carve out my own path, even if it didn't look the way everyone else's did.

So I leaned in. I started studying everything about the business, both at the place I worked and at the places I admired. What made one restaurant feel alive while another felt flat? Why did some bars have a constant, dynamic energy and others felt like they were just going through the motions? I started asking those questions and then started planning how to build places that answered them.

It helped that the kitchen team at the restaurant I was working at had serious pedigrees: the chef had been the executive chef at Le Cirque 2000, and the sous chef was from Balthazar, which were two of the best restaurants in New York City. These guys really got me passionate about all of it: hospitality and service and food and making moments. It wasn't just about showing up anymore. It was next level. The culinary experience, the beverage experience, the service experience: I lit up learning about each part of the business, and I lit up even more when I saw it all come together.

After that crash course as a manager, I finally found myself in Miami proper. There was a hot restaurant chain, and I joined them as a manager because, well, the place I was working in had just shut down. It went out of business, and I needed a job. But this place—man, they did things different. Way different.

My first clue it was going to be something new to me: As part of the training, they had every new employee read *The 7 Habits of Highly Effective People*. I thought I'd been done with homework since college ended, and here I was, closing at the end of a long shift and going home to read about synergy and networks and the principles of organization.

This place also *cared* about shift meetings. A shift meeting, for those of you who haven't worked in a restaurant or a club before, is where the manager gathers servers and front-of-house staff before service begins for the night and explains what the specials are, what wine goes best with them, and mediates any and all drama among staff. At a lot of places, no one wants to be at the shift meeting, and you can tell.

But it was those shift meetings that got me the most excited. I'd have everyone's attention for fifteen, twenty minutes. I always thought, as a young manager, standing in front of people with twenty, thirty, even forty years of experience—why would they listen to me? I was twenty-two years old, managing people who were twenty years older than me. I needed these people to see me as someone who knew what he was doing and what he was talking about, and so I had to learn: What am I doing, and what am I talking about? Two questions you can never ask yourself enough!

I found my edge in education. I'd go home and study. I would *obsess*. What's port wine? Okay, it's a fortified wine from Portugal. When do you drink it? After dinner. Where does it come from and why? Is one better than another and why? Is one more expensive than another and why? I'd make handouts with a breakdown of the port wines we stocked and what I thought servers should know about them. For example, one thing about port wine is that it goes great with chocolate. I'd set up tastings for the servers: a glass of port, a sliver of chocolate dessert. That way, it wasn't just me *telling* them new information—it was me *showing* them new information. It was creating a moment, which in turn let them create moments for diners. When it was time for dessert, they'd be able to explain why port and chocolate tasted so good together. They felt confident making these recommendations, and diners genuinely felt like they'd experienced something new and special. Even back then, I was learning that hospitality is about creating experiences. That's what keeps guest excited, and that's what builds loyalty.

Doing these meetings also helped me realize that a lot of the servers didn't even know what they were recommending or what they were serving, and it wasn't even their fault, because no one had bothered to explain to them before. *What's sour mash in bourbon? What makes a wine dry or tannic?* They didn't know. And I thought, *if they just understood this stuff, they'd be so much more confident. They could sell with more conviction. They'd care.*

I made it my mission to create a culture change. Wine tastings, food tastings, cocktail pairings—you name it. I read nonstop. And I made these little packets to hand out at shift meetings. Every day, before the shift, I'd teach something. And that built trust. Because I wasn't just giving orders. I was giving knowledge that would actually help the servers, which is what leadership is all about. I was giving them a reason to care, and I was giving them the tools to make bigger tips. In turn, I was helping servers feel like they were part of something bigger than one shift or one night, which is something I still hope everyone who works for me feels.

After a few years, I moved to Fort Lauderdale and became the general manager at a place called Velvet Lounge. Back then, it felt easy to bounce between restaurants and clubs and events, especially as I homed in on what I was really good at, which was coming up with big ideas and then making them happen.

That job was where I learned about things that went beyond dinner. Things like content. Events. Brand alignment. How powerful it is to use other people's brands to elevate your own. You book a certain DJ, you get a certain crowd. You throw a theme night, you shape the energy. That was my foundation in events. I learned the sponsorship game there, too. I had absolutely no budget—but I had vision. I pitched Moët & Chandon, the champagne brand, on this artist I found. He created these sexy, provocative pieces—girls with

Moët bottles, exciting but tasteful. I had him do a collection, launched it as an art event, and boom—there was my first brand collaboration, with one of the biggest names in alcohol. I had figured out a way to use someone else's marketing equity—something I'd continue to do over and over again throughout my career and something I still do today. I realized, you don't need money if you have a story. I learned that doing events at a nightclub keeps people interested—attending an event made people feel like they were coming to something special as opposed to another night out. Even if they were regulars who came every Saturday night, an event made it seem novel, and people would start to look forward to whatever I'd throw next. That was really the point where I started to do events that were bigger than my four walls. I was able to bring in sponsors and partners to help supplement or cover costs, which allowed me to bring in talent and experiences that normally would've been way too expensive. I also learned to bring in partners who already had brand deals with certain artists and musicians. These artists owed a performance, and instead of that performance happening somewhere else, I was able to host it at my place. It struck me that I could actually put brands together in a way that was thrilling for the guest. Guests could see how corporate brands could be woven into nightlife in a way that elevated the experience.

And there was an intimacy factor. Seeing the biggest bands in the world perform in a small, intimate venue instead of a massive arena—that's powerful. It completely changes the way the performance lands, both for the artist and for the audience. That realization really set the tone for what became possible moving forward.

In smaller clubs, especially in second- and third-tier markets, you have to wear all the hats. Marketing, promotions, operations—you name it. And here's the thing: In our world, most people either do marketing or operations. Rarely both. Ops is black and white. Clean, tight, structured. How much money are we making? Marketing lives in the gray. It's about feeling, energy, intuition. How much money are we spending? Mixing the two? That's rare. Now, with my own restaurants, lounges, and clubs, I believe ops should focus on ops. Marketing should focus on marketing. They overlap, sure, especially in nightlife. You can book someone, see it flop, or you blow the roof off, and that does relate to sales and the bottom line. But it's best if everyone has their own lane. Ops gives data. Marketing turns it into strategy. One of the things I learned by doing it all is how important it is to have a roster of subject-matter experts. Part of establishing yourself as a leader, I think, is being able to say, when someone asks you a question you don't know the answer to, is . . . that you don't know! But that you do have someone in your orbit who does know, and you'll confer with them as soon as possible.

For me, being a leader is a huge part of my brand, and at that point in my career, my brand was just starting to take shape. I wasn't just throwing parties—I was getting brands to want to be in my rooms. While other clubs were chasing bottle sales, I had car companies, tobacco brands, fashion labels throwing money at my events. Why? Because I treated my venue like a marketing platform. Not just a party spot. That was key, because you can never depend on the party to keep coming back. You can plan for it, obviously, but you will have off nights. And I did. On more than one occasion, I'd get to work and find that the club was practically empty, that the DJ I'd booked was bombing big time. But because I thought of my venue as more than just a club, I was able to look ahead and understand that one bad night wasn't going to put us out of business. I see a lot of people make that mistake and start throwing everything they can think of at the wall in a way that feels desperate, and one thing other people can always smell is desperation.

Because I was doing things my own way and because that was working, people in town started asking, "Who's this guy doing all this at Velvet Lounge?" I wasn't just booking DJs—I was building a culture. I was making noise. And yeah, it meant I worked pretty much 24/7 and had no time for a life of my own, and it meant I was constantly trying to come up with ways to top myself, which was no easy feat. In retrospect, I was probably spreading myself too thin, but I was young and hungry and I was committed to doing whatever I had to do to make it.

Because I was making noise, South Beach came calling. In the early 2000s, I took over Tantra, this tiny 3,700-square-foot restaurant with grass on the floor—if I think about it for a minute, I can still conjure up the smell of the place after a night of people spilling Cosmopolitans all over the sod. Sounds crazy, but it was *the* spot—a restaurant where every night was a high-end dinner party.

I described it as "bohemian meets luxury." People were raging every night, and it was a wild scene. I took the same approach that had brought me so much success in Fort Lauderdale and dialed it up twenty notches, which is to say I focused on the things that mattered: keeping the vibe fun, keeping the guests happy, and making sure it was a place where you could reliably expect to have a great night out.

I also knew that, now that I was in Miami, I had more competition for attention, which in turn meant I had to work both harder and smarter when it came to keeping my place at the forefront of the conversation. For a lot of clubs, you do this by hosting special events—fashion shows, album release parties, even art installations. Of course, to book events, you have to establish a reputation for booking and hosting great events, which means you have to start actually doing it. I had experience from Velvet Lounge, of course, but Miami was a bigger market with more opportunities.

One day, I walked over to the Versace boutique to introduce myself to the manager. "I run Tantra, and every night I see a ton of people come through dressed head to toe in Versace. Let's do an event together."

Based on my pitch, they agreed to host an event with us. The Versace Medusa-head logo was projected onto the walls, and people were like, "How is he pulling this off?" They were one of the most recognizable fashion brands on the planet, and we were a nightclub. A nightclub people were desperate to get into every night, but still—a nightclub. No one stopped to think that Versace corporate wasn't involved (and to this day, I'm not sure if they even knew!). It was "just" a boutique activation, but no one saw it as that—they saw Versace. I was using their prestige to build mine, because suddenly I was known around the city as a guy who partnered with Versace to throw incredible, can't-miss events filled with models and artists and DJs and the people who wanted to be around them. Every event we had led to another event, because we did what we said we were going to do and we did it well. As time passed and my reputation grew, I got good—like, really good—at getting brands to pay my venues to host events for them, which opened even more doors. I was establishing myself not just as a one-off party guy but as a member of the Miami community as a whole.

In 2003, my friend bought the Sagamore Hotel. It was brand new, right next to the Delano, which was, at the time, the nightlife and hospitality legend Ian Schrager's crown jewel. I knew having a place next to Ian's was a huge gift, especially with New Year's Eve coming up.

New Year's Eve in Miami is huge. People plan trips around it years in advance, and after spending a cold holiday season at home with their families, they're ready to shed the sweaters and party until the sun rises over the ocean.

My best friend was doing the Delano's New Year's Eve party, and I teamed up with some other people in our orbit to do Sagamore's NYE. It was a battle of the New Year's Eve parties.

When I tell you we had everyone who was a big deal in 2003 at that event, I mean it—we really had everyone! We had the late, wonderful DJ AM. We had Samantha Ronson, who is still a big deal in nightlife. Adrian Brody had just won the Golden Globe, and he was the favorite to win an Oscar (which he did, a few months later), but first he was going to spend New Year's Eve at the Sagamore, soaking in his amazing year.

It was going to be the night.

And it was a fucking disaster.

To start, we oversold it—like three thousand or four thousand tickets over. Disaster.

Ran out of ice by 10:00 p.m. Another disaster.

Mud everywhere from the rain. People dancing on top of a Jaguar, which looked kind of cool if you didn't know that the Jaguar was there as part of a sponsorship I'd negotiated with a local dealer and needed to give it back the next day, preferably not dented and scratched from being stomped on by girls in five-inch Manolos.

That night probably took years off my life, but you know what? We dominated the rest of the city's parties, in a good way. We beat every major club in terms of attendance and press, including the Delano, to my friend's annoyance. The people who made it in still talk about what an epic night it was. Having mud from the Sagamore New Year's Eve party all over your designer jeans was a Miami partier's badge of honor.

After that night, Roman Jones at Opium Group and his two other partners, who were nightlife stalwarts and people I really looked up to, asked me to join their team and help them grow. At that time, Opium Group owned some of the most popular clubs in Miami, and they were constantly expanding into new spaces around town. Working there was something every guy who did what I did was aiming to do. I told them that I wanted $2,500 a week to get the job done, which was too rich for their blood. Roman's partners weren't sure I was going to meet their expectations. I remember them saying, "Roman brought you here, but we don't even know who you are, kid." Miami is full of guys trying to make it on the club scene, and a lot of them will tell you whatever you want to hear and then not deliver, so while they knew I had a solid reputation, they weren't about to throw cash at me before seeing what I could really do.

Their counteroffer was $1,500, a full thousand bucks less than I was asking for.

Fortunately, even then, I lived by the rule that you should never sell yourself short.

So I said, "I'll tell you what. I'll do the job for a month at $1,500 a week. And at the end of the month, if you want to keep me, you up that to $2,500 and reimburse me the difference from the weeks I already put in. Or we just part ways, no harm, no foul, all good. I'll be thankful for the opportunity."

Within two weeks, they were certain they wanted me to stay, and I went full throttle bringing in major sponsors, A-list names, and famous DJs every weekend to clubs like Opium and Prive. I ended up taking Opium Group to a whole other level, and that's when I really started to make waves. Guns N' Roses performed; Paris Hilton and Nicole Richie, when they were on the cover of every magazine, threw the launch party for their TV show at one of our venues. We were owning the scene—by this point, Opium, Prive, and Mansion were all clubs under our umbrella, and whether you were a local or just down in Miami for the weekend, you were going there—or trying. If you were reading magazines in the supermarket checkout line, you'd see pictures of actors and musicians and models stepping into our spots, and even people who didn't usually deign to wait in line would queue up for our clubs. But Opium, though it was a juggernaut, wasn't truly mine. And what I really wanted was something I could truly call my own.

I would have been happy to stay and accept an ownership stake at Opium, continuing to do what I was doing and taking a larger role in shaping the future of the business. But despite my undeniable success, they refused to make me a partner. And, believe me, I asked many times. As it happened, there was another group in Miami that had a club space called Cameo, and they came to me and said the words I'd been dying to hear from my bosses at Opium: "We'll make you a partner."

Without too much consideration, and because I was annoyed that Opium Group wasn't recognizing my commitment and my value, I jumped ship. I wanted to show Opium that they'd made a mistake in not promoting me to partner, and in retrospect that was a huge mistake. Not the leaving itself—I always support people looking to do new things at new places, and sometimes the only way to really take the next step in your career is to make that kind of change. I wasn't thinking holistically about my career, though—I said I was leaving because I wanted to be a partner, but I was really leaving because Opium wouldn't give me the partnership I thought I deserved. See the difference? I was being spiteful, not proactive.

At Cameo, I threw everything but the kitchen sink into my new role. The space was amazing—a historic Art Deco theater completely reimagined, with walls covered in graffiti art and not one but five bars, each with its own unique look. One of them was a nod to the place's history as a venue for underground punk rock shows, and another was tricked out to look like something out of the movie *Barbarella*. Christina Aguilera performed a show for us—at this point she was selling out arenas, and to have her in a tightly packed club was a real coup—and I was constantly bringing in new talent I thought was on the verge of breaking out. I hosted Kim Kardashian's birthday party when most of America only thought of her as Paris Hilton's hot friend. I did everything and anything at that place, and you know what happened?

I failed. Badly. Spectacularly!

From the very beginning, my motivation wasn't right. Everything I did was about trying to prove my past employers wrong, to show them they had made a mistake by not making me a partner. My ethics and beliefs weren't aligned with what I was doing. The truth is, when you go into business with spite as your fuel, and when your vision is about hurting someone else instead of building something great, it won't work. I did it for the wrong reasons, and the result was failure.

Later, when I opened LIV, I didn't worry about what everyone else was doing. I just focused on my own business. That's the lesson: When you spend your time and energy trying to hurt others, you end up hurting yourself. Cameo failed so badly that I had no choice but to sell it—and ironically, I had to sell it to the very people I was trying to prove wrong, my old employers at the Opium Group.

That failure taught me a double lesson. First, your intentions have to be pure. Second, life can slap you in the face twice. Not only did I lose my first nightclub, but I also gave my former employers the satisfaction of knowing they had been right about me. These lessons didn't feel good at the time, but now, I'm grateful. When I failed, I took it personal, and I don't know if I'd be where I am today if I hadn't been forced to humble myself back then.

It was also then that I realized nobody is bigger than the brand. At my old places, I thought *I* was the brand. But I saw firsthand that the brand was bigger than any one person. That lesson carried into LIV and everything I've built since. Over the years, I've had people come and go, people who probably thought they were irreplaceable. But the truth is, the brand lives on, and if you build it right, it continues to get stronger. I've had executives leave, and you know what happens? Other people step up. That's the kind of culture you want to create.

The goal in life is to build a brand that survives even if you're not there. If I die tomorrow, Komodo lives on. Papi Steak lives on. LIV lives on. That's the way I've always tried to build: brands that are bigger than any individual.

I could have let failure derail me. But, thankfully, I'd built up enough of an emotional bank account with people in my industry that, even though I'd had a pretty big miss, I still had solid relationships in Miami. I had failed at turning Cameo into what I'd wanted it to be, but people still knew me as a guy who did great work and as a guy who could be trusted. It's because I built those relationships—and tended to them carefully—that I knew something bigger and better would come along for me, and I was right. That something was Jeffrey Soffer asking me to partner with him on LIV in the Fontainebleau Hotel, and nearly twenty years later, it's one of the longest-running success stories in nightlife history.

And if you needed proof that playing the long game and investing in relationships can change your life, I'll tell you. You know how I met Jeff? His father, Donald Soffer, was my old favorite regular at my very first bartending job. As I continued to move up, we stayed in touch, and when Jeff was ready to make big deals of his own, he knew I was someone who had both extensive experience in clubs *and* someone who had been his dad's favorite bartender. It was meant to be.

LIV was special—I should say LIV *is* special, since it's still the best club in Miami and we've now opened in Las Vegas, too. With LIV, I built a brand, and it changed my life.

CHAPTER TWO

BUILDING AN ECOSYSTEM

The Fontainebleau Hotel is one of the most quintessentially Miami buildings—so much so that the original architect was credited with inventing a new style of design called "Miami Modern." Frank Sinatra performed a televised concert there, a special meant to serve as a welcome-home party for Elvis after he got out of the army. It's practically a main character in the 1964 James Bond movie *Goldfinger*, with girls in bikinis lounging around the pool while James Bond tries to foil an evil mastermind.

The Fontainebleau Hotel also happens to sit on Collins Avenue between Forty-Fourth and Forty-Fifth Streets, and in 2008 in Miami, that might as well have been Siberia. The heartbeat of the nightlife scene was below Fifth Street. No one believed people would travel fifty blocks just to party—not when there were too many other good clubs (some of which, remember, were good clubs because I made them so good).

But Jeff Soffer was one of the biggest developers in town, and he spent a billion dollars renovating the Fontainebleau, believing that the combination of nostalgia for classic Miami coupled with contemporary, high-end finishes would be a draw for tourists and locals alike. Since the hotel was considered out of the normal party zone, part of its genius was that it was going to establish itself as its *own* party zone. It would be so fabulous that once you'd checked in, you'd never want—or need—to go anywhere else. That, of course, meant it had to have a club, and Jeff asked me to become his partner. Hence, LIV was born.

My first order of business was figuring out how I was even going to get people to come—again, no one wanted to drive twenty blocks to party. People also didn't want to go to a place that wasn't near other places, especially if they were on vacation—the ability to party-hop has long been thought of as a must, which is why in so many cities you'll see a bunch of bars and clubs on the same strip. And since the Fontainebleau was getting totally renovated, it wasn't a place that was already on people's radars. A lot was stacked against us, and I'm sure people around town were saying we'd never pull it off.

But here's what I saw: The Setai had opened on Twentieth a few years earlier and was crushing it. The W South Beach was opening on Twenty-Second. So in my mind, the "center" of the city was creeping north. The fifty-yard line had moved. It hadn't made it all the way to LIV yet, but it was coming. The city was opening up a doorway, and it was my job to move people through it. If we waited until it seemed like a slam dunk, we'd already be too late. We were going to be pioneers.

* * *

I knew LIV had to stand out, and before we opened, I was racking my brain trying to figure out how to make a lasting impact. My first big idea? Getting the Victoria's Secret Fashion Show to move from New York and LA–to Miami. More specifically, to the Fontainebleau.

Victoria's Secret is a legacy brand that continued, each year, to find new ways to stay at the forefront. You had every major supermodel in the game walking the runway–Adriana Lima, Alessandra Ambrosio, Heidi Klum. Bras made out of diamonds, feathers, you name it. And they always hosted their famous show in either New York or LA, with huge audiences and a TV broadcast that drew millions of viewers.

I started thinking, How do I tell the world we're back? Not just that the Fontainebleau is back, but that we're rewriting the rules in Miami. And not slowly but in one massive, global, unforgettable moment.

I remember walking Ed Razek, the guy who ran the whole Victoria's Secret fashion show, around the property. It was still dirt back in the space I was telling them would be perfect for a runway. A literal construction site! Both of us in hard hats, I looked at him and said, "I need you to do the show here. This is going to be, hands down, the hottest hotel in Miami, and your brand will have already done an event here." I laid it out for him.

"Can you imagine? It's November. The rest of the country is freezing their asses off. And Victoria's Secret is opening this billion-dollar resort in eighty-degree weather, poolside, ocean breeze, palm trees. You can't script that!"

To me, it made perfect sense. But people still thought I was crazy.

One of the guys working for the Fontainebleau at the time pulled me aside and said, "This is never gonna happen. I just came over from Atlantis, and we tried to buy the fashion show. They wouldn't move it—not for any amount of money."

I said, "It's moving."

I guess my pitch was pretty convincing, because they saw my vision and took a chance on Miami—and on LIV.

On November 15, 2008, Victoria's Secret took over the Fontainebleau. Heidi Klum hosted. Usher performed, right on the runway, dancing with the Angels while wearing a custom all-black suit. Each segment had a theme—"Glamour Goddess," "The Modern Superheroes," "PINK Planet." The show looked great, of course, but while America was admiring the models, I was admiring the Fontainebleau and thinking about how many people watching at home would be desperate to visit. It stamped us as *the* place, and it gave us instant brand equity.

The fashion show happened by the pool, and the after-party was at LIV. The club hadn't officially opened yet, but we made it happen. We had the Soffers cutting red velvet ribbons flanked by Victoria's Secret Angels, and it was the hottest ticket in town. That night was the softest of soft openings, and I mean that in the best way. We were packed to the walls with every model, exec, producer, and VIP in town. It was surreal. Neon lights, champagne everywhere, music so loud you felt it in your chest.

That party—that night—put LIV on the map before we ever even opened the doors or took a reservation. It said: This is where the future is. At the same time, it was also me using the tools I'd developed at Velvet Lounge on a bigger scale. I used Victoria's Secret, as a brand, to help activate the brand of the Fontainebleau.

And let me be honest with you: Did we make a ton of money that night? No. Not in the financial sense. But that's not why we did it. We did it for the brand.

Sometimes, the smartest thing you can do is borrow someone else's shine. That's the whole game: strategic association. You grow your brand through someone else's marketing dollars. And Victoria's Secret had the best marketing machine around. They spent millions producing that show, flying people in, designing sets, booking performers, shooting every angle in high def. All we had to do was give them a stage—and then share the spotlight. We leveraged their investment to build our equity.

And look, I'm a hospitality guy. I'm in this to create moments, to build something that lasts. I knew if we could get this right—if we could make people feel something that night—we could build on that momentum for years.

We've done a lot of big events since then. We've hosted parties for the Super Bowl, Art Basel, Formula 1. Actors, musicians, athletes, DJs, you name it. And there's a direct line from the Victoria's Secret show to where we are now, because it told people that Miami wasn't just palm trees and spring break. It was fashion, music, culture, and nightlife—all in one place. Here's how I thought about LIV, and how I still think about a lot of my spots: I'm inviting people into my home and, in doing so, I'm showing them things only I'm capable of showing them. We would have huge DJs perform five nights in a row, or we would do a "Dirty Hairy" party on Wednesdays, which was what we called our hipster party—the "ironic mustaches, cool haircuts and tattoos" vibe kids today call "indie sleaze"—before that scene was big on the club circuit. We were lucky enough that Joaquin Phoenix performed his rap song the second night we were open. Guys like Diplo and Chromeo, who are household names now, were considered underground in 2008, DJing at small, scrappy clubs on the other side of the bridge. At LIV, we brought them in and put them in big, glamorous productions. Much like the location, the talent was also looking to the future, and it's always been important to me to operate like that. I was—and still am—constantly looking for new DJs and musicians and artists, and I've learned to really trust my gut. I'm not saying everyone I've ever booked has gone on to become a global superstar, but a lot of them have. At LIV, up-and-coming DJs got to earn their chops playing for bigger crowds, and our crowds got to feel like they were getting in on the ground floor of something special. No one else was doing what we were doing, which made everyone want to be where we were.

I was glad that LIV was a place where everyone wanted to be. It was the anchor. But here's the thing: I started to realize that before people went to the club, they needed a place to eat. And after the club, they needed somewhere to sleep. A nightclub alone isn't enough. So I thought, What if I control all those parts? What if I don't just give you a party, I give you your whole night—your whole weekend? I was seeing it unfold every night myself. Before LIV, I used to gather all the DJs, models, and table buyers and host these big dinners—thirty, forty, sometimes fifty people—at Scarpetta, this Italian spot in the Fontainebleau. And I started noticing something: All the other VIPs would book tables around us. I'm sitting there thinking, "Wait a second. . . . I'm making this restaurant hot just by bringing our crowd in—and then everyone heads to LIV after." They were spending time and money at LIV, but they were also spending time and money at dinner. So I asked myself: What are we doing? Why aren't we the ones owning that whole experience?

That's when I decided to get into the restaurant business, starting with a place called Komodo.

Let me tell you something about Komodo. In 2015, Brickell, the downtown Miami neighborhood we built it in, wasn't what it is today. Now, you walk down the streets of Brickell and it's luxury hotels and high-end designers' stores and trendy restaurants, but then it was a bunch of empty buildings and a dozen half-finished glass towers. Developers had gone all-in on condos in Brickell, and suddenly the condo market was crashing—people were losing their shirts trying to flip these preconstruction contracts they'd signed. These big, glassy boxes seemed like they were going to sit empty for years. But once the market tanked, those units turned into rentals, and the neighborhood suddenly saw an influx of new residents.

And you know who rents? Young professionals. People who want to live in a happening downtown and go out every chance they get. Also known as . . . the people coming to LIV on a regular basis. The people I built Komodo for were already my guests, and I already knew what they liked. It made perfect sense: If the people who were partying with us at LIV started moving to Brickell, we'd follow them.

Around this time, my friend Noah Tepperberg called me and said, "Hey, there's this restaurant space I looked at. It's not right for me, but it might be good for you." So I walked the space. Nineteen thousand square feet, huge, on the first floor of an office building twenty minutes from LIV and South Beach.

Most people would've passed on it—it's too big, too risky. But me? If I'm gonna open a restaurant, I'm not doing some tiny spot in a strip mall. I'm going big. I had a vision for a place that was a destination—a place people would want to come before continuing the party at LIV, but also a place that could be an experience all its own.

I walked my friends through the space, and they looked at me like I was crazy. "This is gonna be a zero," they said.

Even Jeff Soffer, the owner of the Fontainebleau—someone I'd made a lot of money for with LIV—passed. I thought doing a restaurant together would be a natural progression for our partnership, but he said something I've never forgotten: "You're a nightclub guy," he told me. "You're not a restaurant guy."

That stung.

Still, I was committed to making this work. I raised $10 million, and we opened. I thought everyone would show up. I thought it would be the biggest thing ever. Mr. Cocky Nightclub Guy, right? And then . . . 150, maybe 200 people showed up the first night. That's in a space that seats 350. That place looked empty.

People didn't believe in me. They didn't believe I could do restaurants. So I had to prove them wrong.

When I first opened Komodo, I made the mistake of thinking everyone would automatically show up. I was the owner of LIV, after all. Wasn't that enough? But it turned out a restaurant doesn't work that way. People weren't just going to follow me across the bridge because I said so. Brickell wasn't the center of gravity yet, and in those early days I had to hustle. I guilted people into coming. I leaned on my DJs, on friends in town, on anyone I could. Instead of meeting me at a restaurant near LIV, I told them, "If you want to see me, you're coming to Komodo."

And I backed it up. I lived and breathed that place. Six or seven nights a week, you'd find me there. My team, too—they didn't have a choice. And slowly, it started to work. Komodo became the place where people wanted to be, and the halo effect kicked in. Everyone was coming, and suddenly it was the cool meeting spot in Miami. On any given night, if you weren't at Komodo, you were missing out on the pulse of the city.

The menu was designed to create energy. I didn't want the old-fashioned appetizer–main course–dessert routine. We served everything as shareable plates, four or five dishes at a time, and it turned dinner into a communal event. People didn't eat just with their mouths; they ate with their eyes. We gave them something to look at, to photograph, to remember. Everything was visual, Instagrammable. Komodo was really the first time I saw people dining through Instagram. And in that moment, I understood: Social media wasn't just shaping the way people thought about restaurants; it was moving them, physically, to the door.

That's when I started realizing the power of making the people inside the restaurant into stars. Take the Duck Man—this guy makes the best Peking duck you've ever had. We have a window lined with Peking ducks, and every night I'd bring people over to the window, hand them a bird, and snap a picture with the Duck Man himself. Then I'd blast it all over my socials—Duck Man, Duck Man, Duck Man. Pretty soon, guests were walking in and asking, "Can I take a picture with the Duck Man?" One dish, one character, one photo op—it created a mythology around the place.

Last year? Komodo was the highest-grossing independent restaurant in America. We made $41 million—at one restaurant! And that opened the door to everything else.

We learned pretty quickly that restaurants feed the nightclub. But there's a time gap we had to fill—the time between dinner and when nightclubs in Miami start popping off, which is usually around twelve-thirty. So we started attaching lounges to our restaurants. First, Komodo Lounge. It's a place to get post-dinner, pre-club drinks, which both gives people something to do so they don't lose steam and call it a night and gives me space in the restaurant to seat more diners. That's where it began. The lounge keeps you in our world longer. It turns dinner into a night out before you even step foot in LIV. That's the ecosystem. Restaurant to lounge to club. Keep people in your orbit.

Eventually, I realized, "Why am I sending people to other hotels after they leave my nightclub?" So we opened The Goodtime Hotel in partnership with Pharrell Williams. The restaurant and pool at The Goodtime are always packed, but the rooms are what we call "micro-rooms"—they're impeccably designed, but they're on the smaller side, which makes it a harder sell for a high-end clientele. It's been a great learning experience for me, because it helped me continue to home in on who my guests are and what they want. Opening a hotel also allowed me to figure out another part of the ecosystem: the "day club," centered around the pool. Turning that into a true experience means I keep people in my orbit during a window of time—say, noon to five—that I'd otherwise miss out on.

Hospitality is about experience, and not everything hits. Sometimes I try things, and they just don't work. People have expectations about what they're getting from me, and if it doesn't match up with that energy, with that vibe, they'll bounce.

But that's also a strength. Because it means people trust us. They trust me. They're coming to us for birthdays, anniversaries, bachelor parties. They're giving us their big moments. That's a huge responsibility, and it's not one I take lightly. If someone is coming to my restaurant to spend their hard-earned money, it's important to me that they feel like it was worth it.

From there, we started thinking, "How do we expand this ecosystem into other cities?"

That's when Dallas came calling.

Dallas may not seem like an obvious choice for expansion, but I know my base, and I know how to get them early. We knew, for example, that Vegas would be on the horizon. But Dallas is one of the biggest feeder markets for Vegas—people who live in Dallas love Vegas, so it made sense to go there and establish ourselves as a known quantity.

That's how Komodo Dallas was born. People showed up in droves for the opening. Thousands. They told us it was the craziest opening they'd ever seen. Now, entering a new market is always scary. It's different. You're not on home turf. But the ecosystem travels because the vibe travels. It's my mission that everyone who comes to one of my restaurants or clubs feels like a star. People want that energy. They want to eat something amazing, dance to something loud, and feel totally immersed in the world we've created. That's what we give them.

I think of my clubs and restaurants as upscale mousetraps. I attract people to my house. But what they don't always see is the strategy behind it. The DJ lineups, the energy at the tables, the lighting—it's all choreographed to make you feel something. It's theater.

We're building a world where everything connects. If you come to Miami on a Friday night, you eat at my restaurant, you party at my club, you sleep in my bed, and on Saturday you wake up and lounge at my pool until it's time for you to eat at my restaurant again. I want you living in our world all weekend long. And it works because it's all built around real experiences and real energy.

That's how I think. What feeds into what? How can I link this part of the business to that part? Every move is about synergy. That's why we're successful. It's not just a restaurant or a club, it's an ecosystem built around an entire lifestyle.

And listen, I've made mistakes. Things haven't always worked. But I stayed the course. I didn't get distracted. I didn't chase shiny objects. I focused. When you hyperfocus, you figure it out. I figured out restaurants. I figured out lounges. I'm figuring out what's next.

This is what I know: People want to feel something. They want to feel like they're having the most fun anyone's ever had. That's what we deliver, night after night.

Hospitality is one of the toughest industries to break into, much less dominate. It's fast, competitive, expensive, political, full of ego, and not exactly known for its work–life balance. And let me be crystal clear about something: I didn't have a trust fund. I built what I built by putting in the time. I learned every job—busboy, host, security, manager, DJ booker, event planner—before I ever opened anything of my own. That's the only way I could compete with the guys who did have the money and connections.

I always tell new entrepreneurs: Business is business. The industry may change, but the fundamentals don't. Whether you're opening a nail salon, a gym, a food truck, or a supper club, it's the same playbook. Know your market, control your product, manage your costs, and above all, build something people want to be part of. If you're relying on copying what the guy next to you is doing, you're already behind. You don't chase trends; you set them.

In nightlife, there's always some buzzy DJ or artist everyone's suddenly obsessed with. But if you're booking them after they've already gone viral, you're playing catch-up. The real skill is spotting the ones who are about to blow up. I'm talking six months before the general public knows who they are. You've got to be close enough to the culture to feel the rumblings—watch how people are dressing, what they're listening to, what they're reposting at 3:00 a.m. on Instagram stories. That's your early warning system. What the underground is listening to now will be dominating pop culture in six months, so part of my business is keeping my proverbial—and literal—ear to the ground at all times.

It's a way to keep people in my ecosystem—they want to see what I'm going to do next—and a way to keep my ecosystem growing. As people show me what they're interested in, I can show them what I think their next big obsession will be, whether it's a dish at Komodo or a DJ at LIV or a new product I'm investing in.

As a business owner, your ecosystem is your most powerful resource because it's the resource you build yourself. Buildings can change ownership. Chefs quit to start their own places. "Cool" neighborhoods shift. An ecosystem is something you can take with you, anywhere and everywhere. Take care of it—and the people within it—and it will take care of you.

CHAPTER THREE

BUILDING RELATIONSHIPS THAT LAST—AND WHY YOU SHOULD ALWAYS TAKE IT PERSONAL

I'm a sensitive guy. Honestly! I take everything personal. When Cameo failed, I took it personal. Some people might tell you that "taking it personal" is a bad thing. That it means you're too sensitive. That you care too much.

I think that's bullshit. I think you can't ever care too much. I think you should take it personal.

When I say I'm taking something personal, I'm making the statement that if someone's needs are not met in the way I want them to be, it hurts me. That doesn't mean I get sad and go cry in a corner when something doesn't go my way. I don't mean I let it beat me down. What I mean is I take accountability. I own it. I absorb it. And yeah, sometimes it makes me nuts. But that's what pushes me forward.

When I see someone I'm close with go to someone else's spot instead of mine, or they hit mine once but then spend the rest of their trip all over town? That shit bothers me. Deep down, I feel it.

Because, as we've been over, I've worked for my entire career to build an ecosystem. Not just one spot, not just one night, but a whole world. I want to keep people in my world. And when they drift out, even for a meal, I feel it. I want people to think twice before they go somewhere else. I want them to feel like they're missing out if they're not with me. If I invite you over to my house, I'm going to offer you lunch, and an espresso shot, and as many beverages from the fridge as you want. I'll call you an Uber from my own phone, and if you don't have dinner plans, I'll make sure you've got a seat at one of my restaurants before we say goodbye. I'm a natural host, and that extends from my home to my businesses—feeding and entertaining people is my job and my calling, and it's personal.

That probably sounds crazy to some people. But that's how much I care. That's how I'm wired.

When I started my career, it was a different game. There were only so many restaurants, so many clubs, so many places to go. Now? It's endless. You can eat anywhere, party anywhere, hang out anywhere. There's a new opening every week, and Miami is a hot expansion spot. People open restaurants in New York, they're wildly successful, and so they do a Miami outpost, which in turn becomes a hotspot for Miami's particular mix of locals, snowbirds, and tourists. Everyone's got a moment. Everyone's hot for a second. And that's fine. That's the business. But it doesn't mean I don't take it personal when I open up Instagram and see someone I consider a friend eating at a restaurant that isn't mine.

When someone I know eats at a restaurant that isn't one of mine, I internalize it because it means I must not be doing something right. Sometimes it's as simple as not reaching out, not keeping the relationship going, not saying, "Hey, how are you?" to remind them that my places are where they should be.

My restaurant Papi Steak is next door to a restaurant called Milos, which has a huge front window. Every night I'd walk by on my way into Papi, and I couldn't help but look inside. If I saw people I knew eating there, it hit me in the gut. I'll never forget the time Michael Bay was sitting right at the front of that window. I literally made a cut-throat gesture at him through the glass. That's how personally I took it—my restaurant was next door, and yet he was there, not with me.

I instill this in my team, too. If someone we know is at another restaurant or another nightclub, why is that? Are they not reaching out? Are we not making sure our people feel at home with us? I always internalize that. What could I be doing better to make sure those people are with us?

I'll ask my team, "Why is your friend posting on social media about being at another restaurant and not one of ours? You should let them know how important it is to you that they support you and your pursuits." I certainly do.

Now, just because I fight hard doesn't mean I'm not gracious. When my competition comes into my place, I take insane care of them. Frankly, I want them to leave feeling like they had the best meal of their lives—and annoyed that it was at one of my places and not one of theirs. I roll out the red carpet. Because to me, there's no greater compliment than your competitor choosing to spend time in your place. That's the best feeling—and for the record, I go to restaurants that compete with mine as infrequently as possible.

I'm lucky that my best friend understands how I feel, because he's in hospitality, too: Noah Tepperberg from Tao Group Hospitality. Noah and I have known each other for more than twenty years, and we're very similar. He ran a group of very successful clubs in New York City before expanding into restaurants, and now he's got places all over the world. I think our relationship has been so successful because we've gone through so many of the same things, and we've been able to turn to each other to ask the questions we'd never ask anyone else. Noah and I came up in the business at the same time. As I started doing more events, we began talking about ways to incorporate sponsorships into our own businesses. We've always been able to bounce ideas off each other, and we push each other to grow stronger. What makes our friendship so special is that there aren't many people who see the same things I see every day, who I can go to for advice about handling a tough situation or to figure out how to make a guest feel even more special in my venue.

Beyond business, we genuinely cheer each other on. This industry can be brutal—so many people secretly hope you fail—but with Noah, it's the opposite. He wants me to succeed, and I want the same for him. Our support is real. We fly across the world to attend each other's openings, no matter where they are. That kind of loyalty is rare in this line of work.

It also helps that we've always been able to work with each other instead of against each other. Even in the early days, we were strategic. During the Super Bowl, he would host the Maxim party on Friday and I would host the ESPN party on Saturday. I'd tell him which big names I had coming; he'd do the same. We shared resources so both of our events could be as strong as possible.

Now, decades later, with both of us married and raising kids, our families have become intertwined. Our wives have an amazing relationship, our kids are close, and I have a real, true friend—and mentor—in Noah, and he has one in me. In an industry where authentic friendships are hard to come by, I consider myself lucky to have him.

We're now partners in a spot called Casadonna, a restaurant in Miami. We talk ten times a day—sometimes more.

I take my relationships just as personal as I take my business, because if you only show up for people when it benefits you, that's not a relationship. That's a transaction, and it's important to know the difference.

That's why I check in. That's why I stay on top of my people. Because I know how easy it is to lose touch. To assume everything's fine because the last time you saw them, it was all good. But life moves fast. People move on. Loyalty is earned, and it has to be earned again over time. I take that part very seriously.

* * *

I once bought a boat from a friend. Actually, the guy wasn't just a friend—he was also my business partner. At the time, it seemed like a straightforward deal. It was a government-seized boat, and I got a great price on it, well below market value. But later, I found out that he had made a million dollars on the transaction. It wasn't the money that hurt—it was the feeling that someone I trusted hadn't been up front with me. The fact that he profited without telling me cut deep. It was personal. That lack of transparency changed the way I approach every deal and relationship to this day.

I remember thinking about it over and over. If he had just told me, it would have been different. "Here's this deal," he could have said. "You're getting a great price, and just so you know, I'm making X on it." I probably would have done the deal. But because he didn't tell me, it felt like a betrayal. I do so much for people without asking for anything in return, and here was someone I trusted who was doing the opposite. That hurt shaped me. Now, if there's any kind of money involved in a deal with a friend or partner, I make sure everything is transparent. No surprises. No hidden agendas.

It wasn't just about the boat. It's about the way I run my business and approach relationships. I want to help people help themselves. I play the long game. I do things for people I care about because I genuinely want to see them succeed. I don't have a hidden agenda. In hospitality, the lines between friend and business associate often get blurry because they often *are* blurry. I've gone into business with a number of friends, and I also have plenty of business associates who have become my friends. That's why transparency is really important to me.

I've always made it a point to be very transparent, especially when there's any kind of transactional element involved. That line between personal and business can get blurry, especially in the world I live in, but I've learned that as long as you're up front, honest, and communicative, you can avoid so many problems before they even start.

I've been friends with Kim Kardashian for almost twenty years. She's a loyal friend and a great entrepreneur, and we've always been interested in watching each other succeed. The first time I met her, when she came to one of my clubs with Paris Hilton and their whole crew, I just had this feeling about her—it sounds corny, but I knew she was going places, and we stayed in touch. I hosted parties and events for her, and she always made sure to call me and come to my places when she was in town.

I once connected a friend with Kim Kardashian on a CBD deal. Later, the person my friend was working with said he wanted to give me 5 percent of the company as a thank-you for making the connection. Even though it didn't affect Kim's deal at all, I felt compelled to ask her permission first. I called her and explained everything: "The deal's done; it won't affect your earnings, and this is purely a gesture of thanks." She appreciated it. She said, "So many people push me toward deals or restaurants because they stand to gain financially, and I find out afterward. It really hurts my friendship. The fact that you came to me and explained it means a lot." That moment reinforced for me the power of honesty and integrity.

Transparency is personal. It's about being yourself and showing people your intentions are clear. When people know you don't have a hidden agenda, it builds trust. And trust is slow. It's earned over time, and it's destroyed instantly if there's secrecy. That million-dollar lesson with the boat taught me empathy, too—understanding how someone else might feel when they realize there's a hidden benefit in a deal. That's why I'm almost obsessive about being up front now.

If I make a connection, broker a deal, or introduce someone to an opportunity, I think first about how they'll feel. Will they feel respected? Will they feel taken advantage of? Is there anything I haven't disclosed that might later hurt them or our relationship? I'd rather overcommunicate than let someone feel blindsided. Because I've been there. I know what it feels like.

I've also realized that these moments shape your business ethos more than any strategy or plan. I don't just want people to succeed because I helped them; I want them to feel safe and respected while doing it. That's what trust is—more than just a handshake or a signed contract. It's knowing that the other person doesn't have a hidden agenda and that their intentions are genuine. Once trust is broken, it's nearly impossible to repair.

That's the way I operate. I never want someone to hear that I somehow profited from something involving them without them knowing about it. That's just not who I am.

To me, it's about staying aboveground. Always. When it comes to relationships, I believe it's always better to be clear, open, and transparent. That way, there are no surprises. No awkward moments down the line. No one finding out from a third party that you were involved in something or got something out of it that you didn't disclose. Because when that happens, you lose trust—and trust is everything.

It's also about keeping the business lane and the personal lane separate enough that you can maintain boundaries. It doesn't mean you can't do business with friends or that you can't have personal relationships with business partners. You just have to be open about it. Say what's what. Be clear about who's getting what, why, and when. And if there's anything that could be misinterpreted or misunderstood, you address it head-on. You don't wait until someone finds out on their own.

I think transparency is the foundation of any real relationship. And I don't just mean romantic relationships or deep friendships—I mean any relationship where there's trust involved. Especially if you're building relationships with people who have something to lose—reputation, brand, influence—you owe it to them to be up front about your role and your intentions. If you have a hidden agenda, the whole thing starts to feel fake, and people can feel that. They know. You might think you're playing it cool, but eventually, it comes out. I have what I like to call "club sense," which means I can tell if someone in the club is spouting a bunch of bullshit. The nightlife world is filled with people who give fake compliments and make fake promises, and I steer clear of them. I'm all about people building relationships with people they trust. And that trust comes from knowing that you're not going to take advantage of the situation. That you're not going to try and turn everything into a profit center for yourself. That doesn't mean you don't make money or do deals or benefit from connections—you absolutely do. But you do it the right way. The honest way. The respectful way.

And honestly, people remember that. I can't tell you how many times someone has come back to me months or even years later and said, "You know, I appreciated the way you handled that," or "Thanks for looping me in back then." That's what builds long-term relationships. That's what keeps doors open. Now when I meet someone new I'm interested in doing business with, I know, when they ask around about me, they're going to hear loudly and clearly that I'm a fair, honest guy.

As I've said before, relationships are currency. But if you're not transparent, that currency is counterfeit. It might work in the short term, but eventually it gets exposed—and it's worthless. Transparency is what gives your relationships value. It's what makes people want to keep working with you, keep showing up for you, keep referring others to you. Because they know you've got integrity. You do what you say you're going to do. And when something comes your way, you communicate.

Another way I show care in my relationships is through adding value. I always try to add value to people's lives without looking for anything in return. When you do stuff for people who may not be able to do anything for you, it changes something in you. This attitude has really steered me in the right direction in my career and in my life. To me, adding value can be as simple as me making your day a little easier or showing you something I know you'll think is cool.

For a long time, when people would come in from out of town, I'd take them on these unofficial little tours through a neighborhood in Miami called Wynwood—just walking around, checking out the murals, popping into random studios or makeshift galleries. It was really casual and informal, but every time I did it, the people I brought felt something. They'd never seen that side of Miami. They were expecting palm trees, beaches, maybe a club or two, and here I was showing them this gritty, beautiful part of the city—full of color, of energy, of graffiti, of soul.

I wasn't doing it to impress anyone. I just genuinely loved the neighborhood, and I wanted to share it. I loved the art, the vibe, the chaos. I even got married there, that's how much Wynwood meant to me. And because I was sharing something that I really connected with, people felt connected to me, too. That's what it was about—showing them something real, something different. No scheming, no overthinking, just saying, "Hey, here's this thing I love. Come see it."

And in those two hours—just walking, looking, talking—our relationships would grow. People often ask why I'm thought of as a true Miami guy, and I think this, as much as my businesses, is the reason why. If you're in town, I'm going to make sure you really see the town—I'm going to tell you where to eat (my restaurants, obviously), what museums to go to, even the best way to get from your hotel back to the airport. Now, Wynwood's changed. It's more commercial now, and a lot of those artists who, once upon a time, were mostly working on exposed concrete walls, are doing big museum pieces and making real money working with brands. For people who walked around in Wynwood with me ten years ago, it's something they'll always remember—that I cared enough to show them something I thought was cool and that they saw it before it became what it is today.

I love being the best connector in the world, and I love to be people's cheerleaders. If you follow me on Instagram, you'll see that almost every day of the year, I'm posting about someone's birthday—if we've met and there's a picture of us together, I'm probably going to post about your birthday! It's just something that makes people feel good—it reminds them that I'm a friend who wants the best for them. In the same way, I love to hype people up. If you've got a new business venture, I want to post about it, come to your launch, try your product. It's the kind of thing that feels good to do, and it also feels good to get that in return. There's honestly nothing greater to me than when someone shows up and posts something—whether it's a congratulations post, they come to one of my openings and share that moment, or they share a new product I'm investing in or a collaboration I'm doing with a brand. That, to me, means everything. It's not even about the press or the hype. It's about the gesture. It's someone taking a second to say, "Hey, I see you. I see what you're doing. And I'm celebrating that." Because listen, a grand opening is a grand opening. It looks fun, but for people who regularly walk red carpets—especially when they're at "household name" level—it's a pain in the ass. I know it is. They're going to walk in and instantly get hit with a thousand flashing lights. Paparazzi outside, fans waiting around the block, everyone with their phones out, trying to catch a glimpse. It's chaotic. And they know it. So when they still choose to show up? That means something. It's easy to repost a flyer. It's easy to shoot a quick text saying "Congrats." But when they actually pull up? When they take time out of their night, knowing full well what they're walking into, just to support me or celebrate a win? That's huge. I've been doing this long enough to know who's really down for me. I pay attention to that. Not just who shows up when things are great, but who consistently puts their name next to mine—especially when there's nothing in it for them. That's what real support looks like. I know what it takes. I know how busy they are, how many requests they get a day. So when they choose to celebrate one of my successes, I don't take that lightly. I'm grateful. And it makes me want to show up for them, too. Because that kind of support? It's rare. And when you get it, you hold on to it. You return it. That's how relationships in this business survive. Not just through deals or contracts but through mutual respect, shared wins, and real, consistent loyalty.

Every time I meet someone, every single time I have an interaction, I try to make sure they walk away with a good feeling. Even if we're dealing with something negative, even if it's a tough conversation, I still want them to leave thinking, "Okay, that was handled well." If they don't? If I know they didn't? Then I go back. I find that person, and I try to fix it. I've done that many times. If I fuck something up, you're going to get an apology from me and I'm going to mean it.

At the end of the day, relationships are everything. And the ones that last, the ones that matter, come down to how you make people feel.

Over the years, I've realized that if you want to build something that lasts—whether it's a brand, a business, a team—you have to start with relationships. Not just building them but maintaining them. Nurturing them.

In my experience, the axiom that people don't remember what you say but they do remember how you made them feel is true. If you made them feel seen, heard, respected—even just for five minutes—that sticks with them. That's what opens doors later. That's what brings people back around years down the line, when you least expect it.

CHAPTER FOUR

WHY YOU SHOULD PLAY THE LONG GAME

I want my relationships and partnerships to last forever and to keep blossoming in new ways, and that's why I play the long game.

Here's what playing the long game isn't: doing things with the express purpose of getting something in return later down the line. The long game isn't throwing in someone's face that you did a nice thing for them, and it's not calling people and saying, "Hey—you owe me." That's having a hidden agenda, and nothing is less appealing to me.

So what is the long game?

It's recognizing that everything, eventually, comes full circle and that you will, throughout your life and career, have the opportunity to be part of so many great things, many of which will happen when you least expect it.

In the club business, I've seen a lot of people make mistakes after a big night. They're so busy celebrating that they forget they've got to do it all over again tomorrow. The key is having the discipline to celebrate the victory while also recognizing that you need to keep going—to win the next day and the day after that. You can't just rest on one big night. Success is constant effort. For me, playing the long game is far more effective than chasing overnight success, and what it leads to is much more valuable.

When I opened LIV, Swedish House Mafia was the hottest DJ act in the world, and they had a manager named Amy Thomson. Everyone who worked with Amy hated her since she was always pissed off and screaming at someone. But she never did that with me. We got along really well because when I said I was going to do something, I overdelivered, which is rare in nightlife. There's nothing people hate more than someone who overpromises and underdelivers or just doesn't deliver at all, and in our business it does happen—a lot of people make promises they can't keep. I also knew that the things Amy was asking of me were for the benefit of her talent, so she was just doing her job, which I respected. I've always been interested in maintaining good relationships with managers and talent—I want the people who DJ at my clubs (and the people they work with) to be happy! Still, enough people complained about Amy that, ultimately, she was fired by Swedish House Mafia. People turned their backs on her, but I invited her to my house for Thanksgiving, and we had a big holiday dinner with my family. I publicly showed that she was my friend. It's my belief people have their ups and downs. It's easy to be in someone's corner when they're on top, but I think it's equally important to be the kind of person who doesn't disappear when someone hits a rough patch.

I helped her get clients. I knew she was great at what she did, so I played the long game with her.

Well, guess what? Sure enough, Amy got back on her feet and Swedish House Mafia rehired her, as did many other artists who'd abandoned her in the wake of her firing. When you're on top, everyone wants to be your best friend. But Amy doesn't remember those people. She remembers me—the person who supported her when she was down and out. She remembers our Thanksgiving dinner, and she probably always will. That's why, when she has new talent, I'm the first person she comes to. Part of success is surrounding yourself with people who are good at what they do, and when I find someone like that, I hold on to them.

There's a phrase people love to throw around: "All press is good press." I couldn't disagree more. I hate negative stories—and I always have. No one likes to see anything negative about themselves, especially in the press. They just don't. I've lived through it, and I've seen what it does to people, to brands, to trust. So when people say any attention is good attention, I advise them to be careful what they wish for. If you're in this game to build something long-lasting, something meaningful, then no, not all press is good press. Some press burns bridges you can never rebuild.

It blows my mind how many people in my industry still haven't figured that out. Some of my competitors think the best way to get press is to leak a story about someone doing something wild or scandalous at their venue. They see the headlines, they see the clicks, and they think they've won. But they don't realize that they've actually lost. They've played a short game and killed the long one.

Here's what they don't understand: Celebrities (and their teams) aren't idiots. They know when a story gets out, and they know where it came from. When something negative leaks about them, especially something tied to a specific venue, they're not just blaming the journalist or the paparazzi. They're blaming you. They know it came from inside the house. And then it's not just one person who's mad—it's their whole team. Their manager, their publicist, their agent. And that team? They don't just represent one person. They represent ten, twenty, thirty other clients—big names, names you want in your building. But now? They're not sending anyone to your club. They're done because they know you're not trustworthy.

And that's where the real damage is done. Because the one juicy story you got? That's over in a day. It's a headline, and then the next story happens and it's gone. It's easy to think things will blow over and be forgotten about. But those relationships? Those don't come back so easily. You've lost trust, and in this business, trust is everything. You can't put a price on it. You can't just buy your way back into someone's good graces. If people don't feel safe in your space—if they feel like you're going to sell them out for a headline—they're never coming back. And they're definitely not bringing their friends.

That's why, when it comes to the press coverage of my venues, I've always tried to look beyond whatever might be happening now and anticipate what might be happening in the future. I've always thought bigger picture. I'd rather miss the moment. I'd rather not have the story go viral. I've seen it over and over again—moments that could've made big splashes in the press, stories that would've popped on social media. But I let them go. I let them go because I care more about what comes next than one moment that no one will remember a month from now. That's what the long game looks like. It's restraint. It's knowing when to let go of the quick win in favor of the bigger picture.

Because what does a quick, sensational story really say about your venue or your business, anyway? That the party got so crazy that people lost control? That so-and-so hooked up with someone they weren't supposed to and now it's splashed all over the internet? Congratulations—one of those "guess who was spotted canoodling" stories means you've now got two big names in the same headline. Maybe it even made the front cover of a tabloid. But what does it actually do for your business? It doesn't elevate your brand. It doesn't build credibility. If anything, it undermines the whole atmosphere you're trying to cultivate. And now two celebrities and their teams are pissed at you!

I'm not interested in being the venue where chaos happens. I'm interested in being the venue where people want to be. Where they feel protected. Where they feel respected. That doesn't come from chasing drama. That comes from building relationships and valuing them. I think this applies to a lot of businesses. When I work with start-ups, I'm interested in people who are at the top of their games, but I'm not interested in people who are tearing down other businesses. Devaluing relationships is also dangerous in a world where everyone knows everyone. That's the part that gets lost in the "all press is good press" mindset. People forget that relationships are the real currency in business, which I know I've already said in this book ten times and will probably say ten more times before the end of the final chapter. Every time you protect someone's privacy, every time you choose integrity over attention, you're investing in that relationship. And those investments pay off. They show up in repeat business, in trust, in long-term loyalty.

I've seen it play out again and again. The people who chase fast press burn out fast, too. They get one big moment, and then they're gone. But the ones who nurture relationships? They build empires. They get the callbacks. They get the deals. They get the second and third and tenth opportunities. That's how you last.

You never know where someone's going to end up, and remembering that has paid off for me in huge ways. If you treat someone like shit, they remember that, too. But if you always show up with respect, you build something that lasts. You also continue to put it out into the world that you're a stand-up person and someone people want to know and be in business with.

That's just been a truth for me from the beginning. One of the best examples of that is my longstanding relationships—personal and professional—with Steve Aoki. He's been with me since the very beginning—like, nineteen years ago, back when I first opened LIV.

At the time, the kind of music he makes—electronic, indie, whatever you want to call it—was not mainstream the way it is today. Not at all. But we believed in it. We believed in Steve, and we believed in the importance of not just playing what people want to hear now but in trying to predict what they'll want to hear in six months.

Now, of course, Steve is a household name around the world, and I know he remembers that I'm someone who believed in him before everyone else did. And what's cool is we've both grown over time. There have been moments when my brand was bigger than his, and I used that leverage to help push him up. Now, he's one of the biggest DJs in the world—still growing, still moving, still killing it—and we share deals and ideas and tips. We're always checking in, making sure each of us is part of the next opportunity. That's what the long game looks like when your relationships are authentic. You're not just helping someone when it benefits you directly. You're investing in their future, and they invest in yours. It creates a special relationship where you're able to vouch for each other's character—when Steve was getting started, booking gigs as often as he could, he knew I'd always be happy to tell anyone who asked what a great DJ and person he was. In turn, if DJs were wondering about what clubs they should be trying to get into and who in the nightlife world they could trust, someone like Steve is unreservedly able to tell them that David Grutman is a good guy.

I remember when Sebastian Ingrosso from Swedish House Mafia first called me about Alesso. He said, "I have this great kid I'm working with. He doesn't even have a logo yet, no branding, no nothing. We're going to have to make it all from scratch."

I said, "Okay. If you believe in it, I believe in you." And we did it. I got involved, helped shape the visual identity, the positioning, the whole thing. And now? Alesso is one of the biggest gets in nightlife. Sebastian is someone who has been in my life for a long time—years and years. We've both grown in our own ways, but I've been there throughout his entire career, and he's been there for mine. These are relationships built on time, mutual respect, and consistency. That's the long game again—trusting the people you trust and investing early. I've met so many people where I've liked their vibe, or their talent, or their product, and that alone is enough for me to want to start to build a relationship. A lot of people wait until someone has something clear to offer before they invest in the relationship. That, to me, is transactional in the worst way. It's saying "I'm only trying to build a relationship with you because of what I think you can do for me." I remember the first time I really noticed the DJ John Summit. He built a huge community of followers online, and every new track he released sparked genuine interaction from that community—likes, comments, real engagement. I knew this was someone worth investing in.

I decided to take a big bet. I signed John to a three-year deal, not because we were following trends but because I saw the potential to create something bigger. My goal wasn't just to put him on the map—it was to amplify the community he had already built and give him opportunities to grow beyond it. I made sure he was seen alongside people who could elevate his profile: Tom Brady, David

Guetta, Lenny Kravitz, Michael Rapino from Live Nation. I captured those moments and shared them widely, letting the world see all the people who were coming to John Summit's shows. Slowly but surely, it helped position him as one of today's most influential DJs.

I remember when I first heard about a new artist from Puerto Rico named Bad Bunny. He was getting a lot of buzz, and I could see why—he had that rare mix of talent, charisma, and drive. I've always trusted my instinct when it comes to spotting potential, and this time, it told me he was going to be huge. When we finally met, we instantly clicked. He was funny, grounded, and focused on building something lasting. I knew I wanted to support him, not because I expected anything in return but because nothing makes me happier than helping people connect and grow.

That's a big part of who I am, especially in my work as an entrepreneur in hospitality. Whether it's through my restaurants, clubs, or ventures, I'm always hosting, always bringing people together. Around the time I met Bad Bunny, my friend Drake was in Miami recording his album *Scorpion*. We met for dinner, and as we caught up, Drake asked me who the most exciting new artist was. Without hesitation, I said, "Bad Bunny."

I had Bad Bunny's manager Noah Assad on the line and told him, "Drake wants to do a song with Bad Bunny." He was skeptical. "Everyone says that, but nothing ever happens," he said. I handed the phone to Drake, who told Noah himself, "If you don't come here, I'll come to you."

The next day, Bad Bunny and his team flew to Miami. But things got bumpy. After landing, they found out Drake had to delay their meeting due to a last-minute recording session. Understandably, they were disappointed. They were sitting in my backyard, looking at me like I'd made the whole thing up. My wife, Isabela, ordered pizza to break the tension.

That night, I got a call. "Drake wants to have dinner with Bad Bunny tonight at Komodo," his team said. I passed on the message, and the mood shifted instantly–they cheered. We all went to dinner, and the connection between Drake and Bad Bunny was instant. They decided to record a song together called "MIA."

Though the song didn't make it onto *Scorpion*, it was eventually released as a single, and it became a massive hit. A few months later, Drake was back in Miami for a rescheduled concert. Over dinner, I asked him, "Why isn't Bad Bunny performing with you? The song is huge–people would lose it."

Even though Bad Bunny had just landed in Las Vegas for the Latin Grammys, his team turned around and flew straight back to Miami. That night, when he hit the stage with Drake, the crowd went wild. It was one of those moments that reminded me why I do what I do.

Later, when Live Nation's president, Michael Rapino, asked about artists in the Latin market, I connected him with Bad Bunny's team.

What came next meant the most to me. When Bad Bunny was about to sign the Live Nation deal, he had one request: "I want to open a restaurant–and I want to do it with David Grutman."

Shortly after, I got a call: "Would you do a restaurant with Bad Bunny?"

My answer was immediate—yes.

That's how Gekkō was born. We opened on August 11, 2022, during Miami's slowest season. Everyone said it was the worst time to launch anything. But opening night proved them all wrong. The street outside was packed. Thousands came out. The energy inside the restaurant was electric.

For me, it wasn't just about launching a successful spot; it was about what it represented. A connection that started with no expectations, just a desire to help someone grow, had led to something beautiful. That's the power of bringing people together for no reason other than to see what might happen when you do.

There's this idea floating around in business that every deal needs a winner and a loser, that for one person to come out ahead, the other has to take a hit. That's not how I work. I believe in the win-win, and I think it's one of the biggest reasons I've been able to build real relationships in this business—not just transactions.

If I walk away from a deal and I feel like I crushed the other person, like I took them for everything, that's not a win-win. That's not going to build trust. That's not going to build anything lasting. I'd honestly rather lose money on a deal than damage a relationship.

It's the mindset I have when I'm negotiating with landlords. These days, they're coming to me: "Can you open something in my space?" Landlords I work with know that they can count on me to

83

activate a space. I can come into a neighborhood that hasn't taken off yet and put it on the map. That's also a win for me.

And sure, I'm going to negotiate a smart deal for myself. Let's be clear—I'm operating a company, not a charity. But I also never want that landlord walking away from our deal thinking, "Wow, Dave took advantage of me." That's not how I move. That's not how I want to be remembered, especially in my own hometown, where I know I'm going to be opening new spots for the next thirty years.

The way I see it, every time you sit down to do business with someone, you have an opportunity to show them who you are. You can show them that you're out for yourself, or you can show them that you understand how to create something that benefits everyone involved. I always try to be the latter. It would be easy for me to insist on always having the last word, on always earning a dollar more than the other guy just to say I won. But if I do that, the other guy might not want to do a deal with me next year, and that, in turn, means I've lost. Playing the long game means showing people you're a good partner not just today or tomorrow, but for the long haul. I've found that one of the most powerful tools in negotiation is simply putting myself in the other person's shoes—really thinking about what they're trying to get out of the deal. Sometimes it isn't even financial. It might be a marketing opportunity or a chance to build their brand. Understanding that perspective changes everything. My goal isn't just to get what I want; it's to find a way for the other person to get what they want at the same time. When you approach negotiations that way, everything falls into place much more naturally. If you just charge in trying to push your agenda, ignoring what the other side is after, the deal tends to crumble.

This approach doesn't just help in the moment. Years later, when I might need something from the same person again, that first deal lays the foundation for a better relationship and a stronger footing for round two. It's not just about a landlord or a single business contact. It's about setting up a future where both sides feel like they've won.

I think the real key to all this is your intent. Are you entering the deal trying to screw someone over? Trying to squeeze every last drop out of them? That might work for you once or twice, but it doesn't last. People talk. Reputations stick. And if your name's on the door like mine is, your reputation is everything.

If someone says, "Dave Grutman's restaurant dominated. It's so successful, my long-time guests are now eating there every night," that motivates me. I'm competitive. I love that kind of pressure. But if someone's out there saying I didn't pay them or that I intentionally did them wrong? That's not true. That's not how I operate, and that's the kind of thing I won't stand for.

There's enough room for everyone to win. I really do believe that. But you've got to be smart. You've got to be ready for the challenge. You've got to know when to take the short-term loss for the long-term gain. That's what I've always done.

Here's the thing: When you treat people right, when you take care of your relationships, when you show people that you're playing fair even when you're playing hard? They come back. They remember. That landlord whose deal you didn't gouge? He tells his friend. That DJ you stood by even when the crowd didn't show up? He blows up and never forgets who gave him that shot. That's how the whole machine keeps turning.

It's not about being soft. Don't confuse embracing the idea of win-win with being a pushover. I negotiate hard. I know what I'm worth. But I never want to win at the expense of someone else feeling like they lost. That's not sustainable. That's not real power. Real power is when you can elevate people and still come out ahead.

One thing I love about being a long-game guy is that I find myself seeing great opportunities—and great people and great products—all the time.

Recently, my wife and I were driving through downtown Miami one evening when we passed this tiny pizza place tucked along a quiet stretch of NE First Avenue. We had heard about it—it's called Miami Slice—but we hadn't been yet. What stopped us that night wasn't the smell, wasn't the storefront. It was the line. I'm talking about a line that wrapped around the block, snaking past storefronts and parking meters like it was a club, not a place to get a cheese-and-pepperoni slice.

I've seen lines. I've worked in hospitality for years! I love lines when they're outside my own clubs. But this was two and a half hours deep on a humid Miami night, people sweating and smiling, just to get a taste of this pie.

I turned to my wife and said, "This is crazy. I gotta meet these guys."

So I did what I always do when something sparks that entrepreneurial curiosity in me—I reached out. I got them to come to my apartment, and we just sat down and talked. No pitch, no plan, no contract. We just talked. About entrepreneurship, about what it means to build something from scratch, about passion and legacy, and all the stuff people forget when they're chasing money. They told me about how they wanted to elevate New York–style pizza—not by adding truffle oil or foie gras or whatever, but by perfecting the fundamentals. The dough, the cheese, the sauce, the timing. Everything. They made six styles of pizza, total. That's it. And they didn't let anyone walk in off the street and grab a slice at noon. No lunch service. They open at five o'clock, and then you wait.

Let me tell you, it's the best pizza I've ever had. Times ten. And I've had a lot of pizza. It was like . . . pizza omakase. Like at a sushi counter, when you sit down and let the chef take the lead. That's what it feels like at Miami Slice. And a little while after I tried their pizza and learned their story, I found myself in the middle of something else entirely. Fontainebleau Las Vegas—the home of LIV in Las Vegas—was getting ready to sign a lease with Joe's Pizza out of New York. And Joe's is a classic, don't get me wrong. But I couldn't stop thinking about Miami Slice.

So I said, "Hold up. You need Miami Slice. You need these guys in your place."

I brought the owner of the Fontainebleau to dinner with a couple of friends, and we sat down with the Miami Slice team. I watched the Fontainebleau owner take that first bite, and I could see the change on his face. Pretty soon after, Fontainebleau signed with Miami Slice, and now next time you're partying at LIV in Vegas, you can leave the club when it closes and get a hot slice of the best pizza you've ever had. And that deal? It's going to change those entrepreneurs' lives.

Now, let me tell you the part of this story that I think is important. Did I ask for a piece of that deal? Did I say, "Hey, I made that intro, can I get ten percent?" Did I ask for a finder's fee? A referral bonus? Anything?

No.

Because not everything in life has to come with a financial reward, especially when you're playing the long game. I know that might sound crazy in business today, but it's true. Everybody else— and I mean everybody else—would've said, "Hey man, I hooked you up with the Fontainebleau. Where's my cut?" Makes sense on paper. But to me? That's not the long game.

Now those guys—those Miami Slice guys—if I call them and say, "Hey, I need pizza at my kid's bat mitzvah," they're going to show up. If it's six o'clock on a Friday and I decide pizza sounds good for dinner, I can probably skip the two-hour line that still wraps around Miami Slice every night. Playing the long game will pay off ten times over not just in favors but in friendship, in loyalty, in being part of something real.

Every time I see them now—and I mean every time—they say, "Dave, that dinner changed our business." And every time, it makes me proud.

That's the stuff that matters. That's legacy. That's impact. And it's not a headline, it's not a balance sheet. It's about building relationships that go beyond transactions. I don't need a contract to feel good about helping people. When I believe in someone, I go all in. If it works out for them, that's enough for me. Sometimes the best thing you can do in business is help somebody else win. Not because there's a payday, but because it feels good. Because when good people win, we all win.

If there's a pizza in it? That's pretty great, too.

People will always be after quick wins. They want the biggest DJ tomorrow. The hottest party next weekend. But that's not how you build legacy. Legacy is built by making small decisions every day that add up over years. Being loyal. Showing up. Taking a chance on someone early. Not being afraid to say yes to a favor because you know in your gut it's the right thing, even if it doesn't benefit you immediately.

What's crazy is, when you look back, you realize those bets shaped everything. The party no one cared about became the scene everyone wanted to be part of. The unknown DJ became the headliner. The assistant became the manager then the executive. But it only works if you've been consistent. If you've been solid from day one.

I don't think there's a perfect formula to any of this. But I do think if you treat people right, invest in their potential, and keep showing up—even when there's nothing in it for you—that comes back around in powerful ways. That's the game I've always played. I'm not looking for a quick hit or a flash in the pan. I'm playing the long game.

And it's still paying off.

CHAPTER FIVE

CHECK YOUR EGO—BECAUSE YOUR EGO WILL CHECK YOU

One of the biggest lessons of my life came about six months, maybe a year, after I opened LIV. Everything was moving at lightning speed—wild, crazy, nonstop—and I'll admit, I started acting a little too cool for school. I was caught up in the chaos, drinking my own Kool-Aid, feeling invincible. Then Wayne Boich, a friend who's been in my corner for years and has seen my entire journey, pulled me aside. He looked me in the eye and said, "My man, you're not doing heart surgery or saving lives. It's a nightclub."

That hit me harder than I expected. In one sentence, Wayne reminded me of what really mattered, of my place in the world. I was humbled. It wasn't about deflating me. It was about grounding me, keeping me from losing myself in ego. Wayne was right: I was acting like someone other than myself. I was young to be having the kind of success I was having, and in retrospect I was probably, on some level, feeling insecure. Wayne saw that because he was someone who knew the real me, and that perspective has stayed with me ever since. I'm in the fun business, and knowing that keeps me human. It helped me remember that people like me when I'm being myself, and I try to never lose sight of that. Wayne is deeply respected by a lot of people—including me—and his taking the time to be honest with me like that was a gift. That's real friendship.

Around that same time, another moment made me pause. I had brought Mark Cuban to the DJ booth on a night when we were packed, and almost immediately he pulled me aside. "Do you ever take a second to appreciate what you've created?" he asked.

Honestly, I didn't.

I was too busy running at full speed, too focused on the next move. But in that moment, I realized the importance of stopping, looking around, and taking in the magic—the energy of a night, the connection with the crowd. I'm so lucky that people choose to spend their time and money in my world, and I never want to forget that or take what I've built for granted.

Those two moments—Wayne's words and Mark's reminder—taught me humility and gratitude. They reminded me to stay grounded, to enjoy the ride, and to never let the highs make me forget who I am. Even in the midst of chaos, those lessons keep me centered, human, and, I hope, help me stay the same guy that people liked in the first place.

I still think about those moments when things are going well and I need an ego check. I also talk about it with other entrepreneurs who fall into the trap of thinking they can do no wrong, or when I see someone who started out as a humble, hard-working person start to act like someone they're not.

Because that, my friends, is something that will happen. If you're lucky, over the course of your career, you'll have a lot of failures, because having the opportunity to succeed means you also have opportunities to fail. No one starts out wanting to fail, but it does happen—yes, even to me.

On a bright morning in September 2021, I stood outside the doors of Winker's Diner, keys in hand, filled with that familiar surge of optimism I always feel when I'm about to debut a new concept. At this point, I'd successfully opened LIV, a nightclub in the Fontainebleau Hotel, and Komodo, a restaurant in Miami, so I felt confident I could succeed with both clubs and restaurants. I was ready for a new challenge, and I was ready to try out a concept that felt more personal. I was convinced Winker's was going to be a winner, and looking back now, maybe that confidence was part of the problem.

The idea had roots in my childhood—in a way, Winker's was forty years in the making. I remember being a kid, visiting Miami Beach with my family, and the magical feeling of walking into places like Wolfie's, Rascal House, and Pumpernick's—some of the best delis and diners in Florida. These weren't just restaurants; they were institutions, places where the pastrami was piled impossibly high, where the servers knew your order before you sat down, where the black-and-white-checkered floors had stories to tell. Those memories weren't just nostalgic; they were foundational to who I became as a restaurateur.

So, when I conceived Winker's Diner, it wasn't just another business venture. It was personal. I wanted to re-create that feeling, that sense of comfort and authenticity, but with an upscale twist that would set it apart in Miami's competitive dining scene. The menu was elevated classic deli fare—the best pastrami you've ever tasted, heaped generously on top of perfectly crafted rye bread, Cobb salads featuring huge chunks of fresh lobster, and smoked salmon served with all the traditional fixings that made my mouth water just thinking about them.

The space itself was a love letter to a bygone era. I'd found this former tire factory, and the moment I walked in, I could envision the transformation. We created an Art Deco atmosphere filtered through a '70s lens, with pristine white tiled floors that gleamed under the lights, ocean-blue upholstered booths that invited you to settle in for a long conversation, and a black-and-white sign that looked like it belonged in one of those spots on the Lower East Side that have been serving Jewish American food for seventy-five years.

Winker's Diner was my baby. It was food I'd grown up eating, in a space I'd passed a million times walking through Miami. I even named the place after my one-eyed cat. How much more of myself could I put into this place?

The first few weeks were promising. People seemed to enjoy the food—and it really was great. The pastrami was everything I'd dreamed it would be, and the atmosphere captured that perfect balance of nostalgia and sophistication. But as the weeks turned into months, a troubling pattern emerged.

After three months of operation, my check average was sitting at around $40, which was not nearly enough to turn a profit. To achieve the quality I'm always set on, I had to charge more money for those pastrami sandwiches—say, $35 instead of $20. I assumed that because it was one of my places, people would pay a premium. While the space was beautiful, the restaurant didn't have the same feel as a place like Komodo, and I wasn't selling enough sandwiches—and that wasn't the only challenge. The other issue at Winker's was that, hard as we tried, guests weren't drinking alcohol, which in the restaurant business is almost always going to be the thing that makes you money. In restaurants, liquor sales are often what make or break profitability. Food costs are high, labor is expensive, and the margins are thin. Alcohol, on the other hand, is a much more lucrative product—I pay wholesale for one bottle of liquor, and that bottle turns into a dozen cocktails I can then sell for $15 each.

I quickly realized that there was nothing I could do to bring up liquor sales. This was a problem I hadn't anticipated, and it was a critical one. Now I wasn't selling enough pastrami or enough alcohol to make the kind of profit I was looking for.

At Winker's, the quality was there, the execution was solid, and the reviews were positive. But it wasn't the kind of reliable moneymaker some of my other restaurants had been. The reason why hit me like a punch to the gut: I had created a neighborhood diner when my brand was built on destination dining.

Regardless of reputation, regardless of what people expect, you have to know when to cut your losses. It doesn't matter if you've already had tons of successes, or if you know the press is going to write snarky headlines about your first big flop, or if your competition is going to view your failure as a leg up for them. Trust me when I say it's better to survive in business and fight another day than to just keep bleeding.

We tried everything we could to make Winker's work. We brought in DJs to create energy and draw crowds. We did insane marketing campaigns and hosted big birthdays to generate buzz. But at the end of the day, Winker's wasn't providing people what they wanted, or expected, from me for a night out. They wanted to be blown away, like they were at Komodo and my other restaurants.

The realization hurt, but it was also, in the grand scheme of things, very enlightening. People look to me for great food, but they also look to me for a cool atmosphere, for an experience that transcends just dining. People save up to dine at my establishments, and they try for weeks—sometimes even months—to get prime-time reservations. Guests come to my places to see stars and to be treated like stars. They want an experience, not just a good dinner. Winker's taught me that lesson in the most expensive way possible.

To be able to narrow down what attracts people to you and your brand and to identify why people want to buy into what you're creating is an essential part of business. Understanding your brand's DNA, what makes it unique and valuable, is crucial for long-term success. I know who I am, what I offer, and what people want when they come to a David Grutman club or restaurant. Knowing that is what allows me to make tweaks and try new things while always staying true to my spirit. That's what I'm doing with Komodo Dallas. I'm relatively new to the Dallas market, and I don't know it in my bones the way I know Miami. I'm doing the research, running tests with different events and menu items and collaborations that will appeal to Dallas specifically, while also maintaining the spirit of Komodo. Because I know what my brand's DNA is, it's easier for me to take that concept and translate it to a different market, Because I've had places fail, I've been forced to do deep self-inventories: what went wrong? What could I have done differently? How will I avoid this mistake in the future? And when I come up with something I think I did wrong, I'm honest about it, with myself and with my team. That's what allows me to keep moving forward. If you're not dealing authentically with what goes wrong, you'll never be able to sustain what goes right.

Let me tell you about Story. It was a club we opened in 2012 that could hold two thousand people a night, with DJs and bottle service and sexy lights and the best energy. It was in a neighborhood called South of Fifth. When Story opened, that area was dead. Nothing was going on down there. But I had this crazy full-circle moment— my very first job was in the same building that housed the club. I had started at the bottom—literally in the building's bottom office. And then here I was years later, the owner. That was wild to me.

To go from being the guy taking orders to being the one giving them in the same four walls was surreal.

But here's the thing: Once Story and, later, Papi Steak and everything else opened and the area started booming, the neighborhood changed. Suddenly, there were luxury condos everywhere, multimillion-dollar buildings, and a different kind of resident. Not clubgoers. Not nightlife people. These were families, hedge fund guys, people who didn't want to hear the bass pumping at 3:00 a.m. or people pulling up in Lambos honking their horns. They wanted silence, and pretty soon they had the ear of the mayor.

So, what did the city do? They voted to move the entire South of Fifth neighborhood to a 2:00 a.m. closing time—no more booze, no more music, no more nothing. In a city where dinner reservations start at nine, drinks in the lounge happen at eleven thirty, and the club really gets going around 1:00 a.m., a 2:00 a.m. cutoff was a death sentence. I fought it. Trust me, I fought hard. But I could only fight so far, because I've got other businesses in Miami Beach. I couldn't let one battle sink the whole ship. When you have a business, and especially when you have multiple businesses, you can't let pride or stubbornness or ego drive your decisions. You have to look at the bigger picture. It's about protecting the ecosystem. So yeah, I went to the meetings, I tried everything I could, but eventually I had to pull back.

And let me tell you, losing Story messed me up more than anything else has. We had a thriving business. Years and years of building it up, booking massive DJs, creating moments that helped define Miami nightlife. And then one day, just like that, the government can shut you down. No conversation. No compromise. One day you're operating at full tilt, the next you're being told, "Sorry, you can't play music past 2:00 a.m."

Mentally, that was one of the toughest things I've ever faced. Because it wasn't just a business to me—it was a team, it was jobs, it was culture, it was a whole machine we'd built. And it all just got yanked. But I had to do the thing that's hardest for any entrepreneur to do—I had to take my ego out of it. I had to take my business mind out of it. I had to just sit with it and look at it from another perspective.

If I'm someone who just bought a $15 million condo and I'm trying to relax on my balcony after a long day at work, do I really want a nightclub next door? Do I want people honking outside, yelling in the valet line, music thumping through my walls while I'm trying to put my baby to sleep? Probably not. And I get that. I hate it, but I get it. And it felt especially unfair because we were there first. We helped build that neighborhood. We made it a destination. And then we got pushed out of it. But life isn't fair.

It sucked for my employees. It sucked for my team. It sucked for me financially. But what are you going to do? You can't kill yourself over the things you can't control. Life is going to throw bad situations at you, and you've got to eat them. You've got to keep going and going and going.

They say when one door closes, another opens. It's corny, but honestly, I've learned that it's true. Maybe not right away, maybe not the door you've been knocking on, but a door that will lead to the next place you're meant to be.

Sometimes wisdom looks like failure from the outside, but it's actually the foundation of future success. I'm constantly learning from my mistakes and, as a business owner, the challenges never end. The Key Club looked great on paper. It had this polished, coastal-American look, and we put a ton into the design—leather booths, terrazzo floors, beautiful lighting, that indoor-outdoor vibe. It was like an upscale supper club, which is a concept I still really like. We thought we were bringing the energy of our other restaurants into Coconut Grove, a neighborhood maybe twenty-five minutes from South Beach. It should have worked. But it didn't. I wasn't familiar enough with the area, and I misread the market.

Coconut Grove isn't transient. It's not South Beach; it's not Brickell. It's families. Locals. People who've lived there forever. And with what we do, we need a mix of local support and tourists coming in and out. That's the magic formula. When a tourist lands in Miami, they're not just scrolling Instagram; they're texting their friend who lives here, "Where should I go?" And if your place isn't on that short list, it's game over. Coconut Grove is a great area, but if you're coming to Miami for forty-eight hours, it's probably not going to be on your agenda, and it's key to my business that people who come to Miami for forty-eight hours feel like they have to be at a David Grutman spot. In Brickell, when I opened Komodo, the neighborhood itself was in transition, so I was able to help shape what the scene looked like. Coconut Grove is already Coconut Grove—I was trying to slot myself into an existing landscape, and it wasn't working.

The hardest part of any failure is letting it go. I didn't want to keep throwing time and energy at something that wasn't going to change. And in this business, time and energy are just as valuable as money. Probably more. So eventually, I said, it's done. Move on. No matter how much I put behind it, it wasn't going to turn around.

Gratefully, on this one, I was able to get out alive because I could see the signs thanks to my past challenges. Experience, even painful experience, teaches you to recognize patterns and make better decisions.

Without a doubt, it bothers me deeply when things fail or when I feel like I've failed. But it reminds me to stay sharp. To own my mistakes, to see people and places and markets, and to never let my ego get so big it turns into a blind spot.

So I keep going mainly because, now that I've been doing this for so many years, I always feel like I have the winning formula and that every idea will execute perfectly. The thing is, thinking you have the winning formula doesn't always mean it's going to be the winning formula. Success can breed overconfidence, and overconfidence can lead to blindness about market realities.

This doesn't stop me from trying new brands or growing fresh concepts, but I'm keenly aware that middle-of-the-road models are not what people expect from me. Instead, they anticipate lavish, high-energy, glossy, fun, exciting restaurants. For this reason, Casadonna—my newest restaurant in Miami—really leans into luxury. It's a great date-night spot, but we also do seafood and martinis I know will look good on Instagram stories. I've learned to lean into my strengths rather than trying to prove I can do everything.

This is not to say that, just because you have challenges, you should throw up your hands and quit. When you know you have something special, you have to stick with it. There's nothing more satisfying than conquering obstacles and coming out on top. The key is distinguishing between temporary setbacks and fundamental problems. The contrast between Winker's and my first restaurant, Komodo, was stark—and educational. There was a time in the beginning when I was genuinely scared Komodo wasn't going to make it. This was a massive restaurant—big overhead, big payroll, big everything—and if I didn't make it work, I honestly think I'd be nothing today. The stakes were high, and the weight of it sat on my chest every single morning.

Usually, restaurants start off with a bang—lines out the door, hype everywhere—and then, slowly, they taper off. The buzz fades, the regulars find somewhere else, and before you know it, the place is running on fumes. I've seen it happen over and over again. But Komodo was different. We didn't fade. We kept going up. And up. And up. And now we've brought that playbook to Dallas and Las Vegas, and I know we'll continue expanding.

So the question becomes: How do you do that? How do you

keep people coming not just for the first six months but for ten years? That's the real challenge.

For me, it came down to one thing: You have to keep pushing. You can't ever think, "We've made it. We're done." The second you believe that, the decline starts. I wake up every day asking, "What's next? What's the new idea? How do we make tonight better than last night?" It's a relentless kind of mindset, but it's the only way I know how to work.

On the surface, it seems like they're similar stories, and there's probably an alternate universe in which Winker's is still open, busy but ultimately propped up financially by my other spots.

The difference between Komodo and Winker's is that, with Komodo, I did see a light at the end of the tunnel because I knew when people did start to come, we'd sell a lot of high-quality steak and a lot of top-shelf liquor. But I couldn't change Winker's DNA and turn it into something it wasn't. Business could boom, but if the check averages wouldn't budge, there was nothing I could do. I learned that it's as important to know when to fight as it is to know when to fold.

Ego is one of the greatest strengths of an entrepreneur, but it can also be the greatest weakness. Even more simply put, don't let pride stunt your progress. Undoubtedly, in the beginning, ego is what pushes people to believe they can create a business and take risks. It's the voice that says, "I can do this better than anyone else," the confidence that drives you to invest your time, money, and reputation in an idea.

But it's a fine line between fueling yourself to do great things and blinding yourself from failure. Managing your ego is an ongoing battle, especially as the successes pile up, but keeping things in perspective is key.

The simplicity of Wayne's observation, all those years ago, was what made it so powerful. He wasn't trying to diminish what I'd accomplished or suggest that entertainment wasn't important. He was reminding me of perspective, of proportionality, of the difference between confidence and arrogance. It was a master class in how to deliver tough love without being cruel.

The upshot is that no one knows it all or will succeed at everything they do. Yes, ego can help you push through the toughest of challenges. When everyone is telling you your idea won't work, when the banks won't lend you money, when your family thinks you're crazy, ego is what keeps you going. But at the same time, when it hinders you from preventing a bad situation from becoming worse, it will be your Achilles heel.

Ego can hinder your willingness to ask for help, but being able to glean advice from a trusted advisor will keep you grounded even when things are going well. The best advisors aren't the ones who always tell you what you want to hear; they're the ones who tell you what you need to hear—even when it's uncomfortable.

Looking back on Winker's Diner, I can see it was a necessary failure. It taught me things about my brand, my guests, and myself that I couldn't have learned any other way. It forced me to confront the gap between what I thought people wanted from me and what they actually wanted. It made me better at recognizing when a concept isn't working and when it's time to cut losses. It reinforced the importance of staying true to your brand's core identity while remaining flexible enough to evolve. Winker's failed because it was too far from what people expected from me, but it succeeded in teaching me lessons that have made every subsequent venture stronger.

Failure isn't the opposite of success; it's a stepping stone to it. Every entrepreneur will face moments when their vision doesn't align with market reality, when their confidence exceeds their judgment, when their ego gets in the way of their wisdom. The key is learning from these moments rather than being defeated by them.

The restaurant business is unforgiving, but it's also incredibly rewarding when you get it right. The lessons I learned from Winker's Diner and from every other time I've failed—about brand identity, guest expectations, ego management, and knowing when to quit—have been invaluable. They've made me a better businessman, a better leader, and, ultimately, a better person.

As I continue to build new concepts and expand my brand, I carry these lessons with me. I'm more careful about ensuring new ventures align with what people expect from me. I'm quicker to recognize when something isn't working. And I'm better at managing my ego, even if it is a lifelong process.

Even experienced entrepreneurs can make mistakes, but the true measure of success is how you respond to those mistakes and what you learn from them.

That's the entrepreneur's journey in a nutshell: a series of bets, some of which pay off and some of which don't, but all of which teach you something valuable about business, about people, and about yourself. The key is making sure you survive long enough to apply those lessons to your next venture.

CHAPTER SIX

ADVANCED HOSPITALITY

I know a guy named Burt Rappaport who has been in the Miami restaurant business since the '70s. One day we were talking, and he pulled me aside and said, "Dave, you see that restaurant over there? There's a light out on their sign, one of the letters. They're going to be out of business in six months." And man, that stuck with me—especially when they did close down, just as Burt predicted.

Now, every time I walk into one of my places, the first thing I do is look up. Are the light bulbs out? Is something flickering? Because to me, that's where it all starts. If a light bulb is out and no one cares enough to fix it, then what else are we not paying attention to? It's the details. That light bulb tells a story. It sets the tone. And if we're not even getting the little things right, how can we expect to get the big things right?

Those little things—they matter. That light bulb isn't just a light bulb. It's the first impression, the energy, the care. If we don't sweat the small stuff, we're done. That lesson from Burt—it's burned into my brain, and it's a shortcut to understanding how I think about operating my individual clubs and restaurants *and* my business as a whole.

I talk a lot about being in the hospitality business, so I think it's time we answered an important question: What is hospitality? I get asked this question a lot, especially when I'm teaching my course at Florida International University.

Hospitality, to me, starts broad but always comes down to the details. There's a famous restaurateur who says that hospitality is how a place makes you feel, and I think that's true, but it's something more. It's about anticipation. It's about understanding what a guest wants before they even realize, and it's about you and everyone working with you noticing things 99 percent of guests will never even see. It's about making sure that when someone walks into one of my restaurants or nightclubs, they're walking into an environment where every single touchpoint—the lighting, the music, the energy, the vibe—is calibrated to deliver an unforgettable experience.

Let's say you're walking into Gekkō for dinner. The valet is quick and friendly. One hostess checks you in outside, so that once you have the velvet-rope moment—of course there's a velvet-rope moment at my restaurants—and it's time to move inside, they're ready to greet you by name.

The server knows your name and, if you've been there even once before, knows your preferences, because I have a system for that. The menu's already been dropped, your water glass is full, the music's at a level where you're nodding your head but still hearing your date across the table. It looks effortless, but what you're feeling is actually me and my team doing our jobs.

When I walk through one of my places, I'm not just checking how many heads are in the room. I'm asking: Is someone's glass full? Are the menus sitting awkwardly on top of their plates? I'm looking at posts on social media, and I notice if someone's whole order is on the table at once, meaning everything was fired at the same time instead of being paced properly.

No. That's not what we do. That's not hospitality. And if I see it, I say something. Every single time. My managers know this. My servers know this. I will stop them midshift and go, "Hey, go back to that table. Fix it."

People love to talk about service like it's the same as hospitality. It's not. Service is transactional. Hospitality is emotional. And when you're in a place like Papi Steak—where someone's easily dropping a thousand dollars on a tomahawk steak—you're not just giving them a piece of meat. You're giving them temperature, sizzle, swagger, ambiance. You're giving them a performance. Everything about that moment needs to scream luxury, and they need to feel it. Otherwise, they'll take that thousand bucks and go somewhere else next time. That's the reality.

And here's the thing: We're not short on competition. You think Miami's hurting for hot restaurants or big nightlife concepts? Absolutely not. There are so many options. I remind my team of that all the time. We work hard. We spend months curating playlists, perfecting menus, creating marketing campaigns just to get people through the door. So don't be the reason they don't come back.

I tell my servers: You're my partner. That's not just feel-good talk. You're taking home 18 to 20 percent on every check. That's your piece of the pie—before I even see mine. I've got to pay rent. I've got food costs, labor, security, insurance. You? You're getting paid off the gross, which means we're in business together. So if you're my partner, you better act like it. That means showing up, delivering, exceeding expectations. Because otherwise, this whole thing doesn't work.

Imagine someone's been coming to Komodo every Friday for two years. They've had amazing experiences ninety-nine times. But on the hundredth time? Their server rushes the apps and mains to the table together. Or the lighting's off. The martini has olives even though they asked for a twist. You think they remember the ninety-nine great nights? No. They remember the one bad one. That's just how people are wired. That one bad experience will undo years of effort. And in the hospitality business, we don't get a second chance. This is true in both restaurants and in nightclubs. I can have a guest come in for years who spends a ton of money on bottle service every time. All it takes is one overzealous security guard—who probably means well, by the way!—telling him he can't be standing where he's standing and, just like that, this guy is no longer going to be one of my regulars.

That's why I'm obsessed with consistency. People ask me all the time, "How do you keep it fresh without letting the quality drop?" And the answer is: The foundation never changes. The core is the same. Service. Attention. Detail. Whether it's a new menu item or a classic, it's got to be executed perfectly. That part doesn't evolve. What evolves is the context—the special guests coming in, the trends we're tracking, the little innovations we layer on top. But the bones? They stay strong.

Some people think the nightclub business is just about showing up at 1:00 a.m. and throwing a party, and the rest somehow happens on its own. I'm here to tell you that's not how it works. Not if what you want is to build a real business.

There's a phrase I repeat so often the people who work with me are definitely sick of hearing it: Daytime makes the nighttime. It's one of the biggest truths in hospitality—and one of the biggest misunderstandings from the outside. LIV doesn't technically open its doors until 11:00 p.m., but I'm working twelve hours before that, and my team is, too.

And when I say working, I mean working. We're curating DJs, holding production meetings, confirming artist riders, negotiating with agents, building out marketing campaigns, planning lighting cues, coordinating dynamic table pricing, rehearsing transitions—there's a long checklist, and if you think that gets done in the few hours before the doors open, you're fooling yourself.

This is what separated me from the pack when I first got into nightclubs. So many of my competitors got into nightlife because they liked to party and wanted to get paid to do it. Most of them wouldn't even wake up until 1:00 p.m. I'm not exaggerating. That was the culture back then. You'd go hard until 6:00 a.m., sleep till the afternoon, and do it all over again. I looked around and thought: This is insane. I saw an opportunity to do it differently.

So I made a rule for myself: Get into the office by 8:00 or 9:00 a.m.–every day. No matter what time I went to bed, no matter how late the party went. Why? Because I knew that if I started my day early, I was already a half-day ahead of the competition. And over time, that gap compounds. This is my business, and these are real assets. How can I expect other people to take that seriously if I'm not, as the leader, taking it seriously?

The Miami location of LIV is only open from 11:00 p.m. to 5:00 a.m., four nights a week, but it brings in over $40 million a year. You think that happens by accident? By just . . . vibing out and hoping for the best? No. It happens because every moment before 11:00 p.m. has been accounted for. When I look around at the people I consider true competitors today, they all have the same attitude. When I look around at the past twenty years and think about all the people I know who said they were going to make it big, or were on the edge of making it big, or even, in some cases, people who did actually make it big for a while, there's a common thread. The ones who got lost in the sauce–of partying, of ego, of thinking just being at the club was their whole job–have largely disappeared from the scene. Part of the reason I'm still here–and still moving forward–is because, early on, I learned to never, ever forget that this is my business.

I've got no problem with having fun. Clearly! I love a great night out. I love energy, I love connection, I love building experiences people talk about for the rest of their lives. But my role isn't to enable chaos. It's to curate joy. And to do that well? You need structure. You need foresight. You need the whole thing built with intention.

That's the directive I give to every single person who works for me: The party doesn't magically appear. It's manufactured. Carefully, thoughtfully, obsessively. It's a product of logistics and timing and detail. You don't get the magic of 1:00 a.m. without grinding at 10:00 a.m. That's how it works.

And honestly? Once people understand that, it changes the way they work. You get hosts who are texting confirmations all day. You get managers who are reading contracts front to back. You get bartenders reviewing cocktail specs at 3:00 p.m., sound guys doing level checks before sunset. That's what excellence looks like. That's the standard.

If you ever walk into one of my clubs and think, "This place just runs so smoothly," I promise you it's because of what happened during the day. Because of the fifteen people who showed up early. Because of the systems. Because someone took the time to print a run-of-show and someone else made sure the risers were set and someone else double-checked the comp list. That's where the magic starts. That's the difference between surviving and thriving in this industry. That's how you build a business that lasts.

* * *

At LIV, where we've got people coming from all over the world to party, it's not just about who's DJing that night—you might be coming to LIV not even knowing who the DJ is because it's someone new I just connected with and I always want to bring something new to my place.

It's about how they're greeted at the door. How they feel walking into the space. It's about whether the table is stocked the way they expected. Whether the energy builds right. Whether the lighting cues hit at the exact moment the beat drops. That's not by accident—it's by intention.

We train constantly. We do shift meetings every single day. Ten minutes on the food. Ten minutes on the service. Ten minutes on the cocktails. Then we talk about the guests. Who's coming in tonight? What kind of mood are they in? What happened last time they were here? Maybe they loved the scallops and now the chef is serving them with a new flavor profile. Maybe they're a huge tequila drinker and my mixologist is testing out a new spicy margarita recipe. Maybe they came here the night they got engaged and now it's their anniversary.

It's all human. This isn't just hospitality. It's psychology. It's vibe management.

And yeah, we make mistakes. I see it sometimes—I'll scroll through Instagram and see someone post a photo where they clearly got their apps and mains all at once. You never want a guest to feel rushed. It's the worst feeling in the world, like you're just another body we're trying to turn. That's when people don't come back.

But the thing is, we're in the human business. There's no way to eliminate mistakes 100 percent of the time. The beauty is how we recover from those moments. That's why I hire people who care. People who can react in real time. Fix the energy. Apologize sincerely. Comp a dish if they need to. Turn the night around.

I think that's why we've been able to scale the way we have. It's not just that we're good at what we do. It's that we've built a culture. A DNA. We don't settle for the bare minimum. The minimum doesn't move people. That's not in our playbook.

One of the best compliments I've ever gotten came from Jeff Zalaznick over at Major Food Group. He looked at me and said, "I don't know how you do it. You move people. Literally. Not just a few. Crowds. From restaurants to lounges to clubs. Nobody else does that." And he's right. It's something I've always taken pride in—not just attracting the crowd but curating it.

Let's be honest: The people are the product, too. Who's in the room is part of the vibe. You go to Casadonna, and it's not just the martinis or the Caesar salad. It's who's around you. It's the energy they're bringing. And I'm constantly moving that energy—through texts, through relationships, through subtle cues. Who's eating at Komodo at nine? Who's heading to LIV at one? Where are they staying? That's part of what makes the experience complete.

And here's something I think younger operators miss: This business is fragile. It takes years to build trust and minutes to lose it. One host who forgets a reservation. One bartender who doesn't know what's in the drink. That's all it takes. That's why we invest so much in training. You ask any of our team members—servers, bussers, bartenders—what's in fritto misto or whether the oysters are Kumamoto or Wellfleet? They know. Because we test them. We quiz them. We drill it.

We even role-play. We talk about the guests before every shift. Who's likely to complain? Who had a bad experience last time? What can we do to make it right this time? We're proactive. And again, we're human. But I'd rather make a hundred small mistakes and catch them than let one big one go unaddressed. If an order comes out wrong, I'm not happy, but I can fix it. When someone DMs me about an experience they've had at one of my places that could have been better, I address it. People will come up to me in the middle of a busy night with a complaint, and I address it. Feedback is an incredible gift—it's someone taking time out of their day, for free, to help me improve my business. I can't stand when someone oversells a guest just to make their own numbers look good.

At Papi Steak, we sell an incredible kosher steak that serves two to three people. I've seen it happen—a server bragged, "I sold four Papi steaks to a table of four tonight!" Yeah? Well, you also ruined that guest experience because they're four people who bought enough steak for twelve. If you had said, "Let me send out two, and if you need more we can always order more," that would instantly create trust. But now, because you pushed them into something they didn't need, they feel burned. You might have gotten them once, but you won't get them again.

You can charge a lot of money for something if the guest feels like it's a great value. But the second they feel taken advantage of, you've lost them. And in hospitality, a lost guest isn't just one table—it's everyone they talk to.

Hospitality isn't just making people feel good. It's building a machine where that good feeling happens on purpose every single time. It's creating a culture where everyone—from the busser to the bartender to the security guard—knows they're part of something bigger. Where they carry themselves with pride. That's the magic. That's the difference. That's what we do.

Oh, the bathroom. Anyone who has ever worked in one of my places will tell you: I'm insane about the bathroom. The number one rule in my world—this is Hospitality 101—is what you do when someone asks, "Where's the bathroom?" I train my entire team to say, "May I show you the way?" And you walk them. You don't point. You don't say, "Back left, past the bar." You stop what you're doing and escort them.

You know how many people I've busted for pointing? I catch people all the time. That little flick of the hand like they're swatting a fly. Nope. Not in my house. I'm like the gotcha guy with the fucking bathroom. I see it across the room and I'm on it. That's how detail-obsessed I am. That's how much it matters.

You ever been to a restaurant with a dirty bathroom? Come on. Disgusting. You think I want to eat there? If they don't care about the bathroom, they don't care about the kitchen. That's just a fact. That's why we have bathroom attendants at all our places. Not just late-night spots. All of them. And not just standing there bored on their phones. You go in, you get gum, a mint, a little spritz. It's fresh. It's clean. It's thoughtful. It's like walking into a high-end car wash. But that's not even the point. We do that to keep the bathrooms clean, yes; but more than that, we do it to make a statement. It says we care. About the little things. About everything.

Because hospitality is built in the details. Not the big showy stuff, not the DJ or the Instagram wall. It's the small things. The things that no one thinks matter until they really, really do.

I walk into my own venues and scan everything. Ceiling to floor. I look up. I look down. I check corners. And now? So does my entire team. Because I've trained them to care about the stuff that other people overlook. That's the difference between a place that survives and a place that wins.

When people talk about hospitality, they want to throw that word around like it just means being friendly. Hospitality is precision. It's pride. It's discipline. It's being able to see the world from the guest's eyes every minute of every day and never getting lazy about it.

So when someone walks into one of my venues, they should feel the full effect of what I've worked to create. Not just because the music's right or the lighting's flattering or the food's good—though all of that should be true—but because everything has been considered. Everything has been touched.

And it starts with me. It has to. If I'm paying attention to whether or not the trash has been taken out, everyone else will, too. If I'm reminding you that we always walk the guest to the bathroom, everyone else will, too. If I can spot a flickering light bulb from across a packed room, the team starts looking, too.

So there you have the Grutman Guide to Succeeding in Hospitality:

Show up early.

Never point the way to the bathroom.

And always, always have a backup supply of light bulbs.

CHAPTER SEVEN

BUILDING THE CULTURE

At the end of the day, you can have the best food, the best cocktails, the best DJ, the coolest design—and it won't mean a thing without the right team. I've been in this game long enough to know that the secret sauce isn't all me. It's not even the concept. It's the people standing next to me. And the people who used to stand next to me at the door, learning from me in real time, are now the ones teaching the person standing next to them. That's the chain reaction I want. It's how the culture passes from one person to another. You can't fake that. I'm only as good as my team, and they're a huge part of any of my successes. I'm very big on growth, and it's a point of pride for me that a lot of my team members have both been with me for a long time and done a wide variety of jobs.

One of my team members is someone we call "Irish Sarah." She came over to Miami from a club in Ibiza—I brought her on board so the DJs flying in from Europe would have a familiar face waiting. She handles contracts, fees, and sometimes spends a whole week with an artist to make sure they're taken care of from start to finish.

I never forget that I got my start as a bartender, and if someone working in one of my places has the drive to grow in this business, I want to support them.

The team is the heartbeat. They're the ones making sure a guest feels welcome from the second they walk up to the rope to the second they leave. They're the ones protecting the vibe, catching problems before they become disasters, and delivering those little moments that keep people coming back.

And building that team isn't just about hiring the right people. It's about creating a culture where they want to stay, grow, and protect the business like it's their own. It's about giving them ownership—real or symbolic—and showing them that you see their value.

Assembling the right team is the one of the most important things you'll ever do. I've interviewed a lot of people over the years—managers, general managers, bartenders, servers, hosts, you name it. One of the first things I look at is whether they hop around a lot. If I see someone bouncing from place to place every six months, I'm already skeptical. It's never worked out for me. I want people who stick, who see the value in building something over time.

Confidence is another big one for me. I like confident people. What I don't like is cocky. Confidence says, "I've got this and I'm ready to learn more." Cockiness says, "I've got this and I don't need to learn anything." That's poison on a team.

And here's maybe the biggest thing: I look for that entrepreneurial mentality. I want people who treat the job like it's their own business. That doesn't mean they're going to run off and start a competitor tomorrow. It means they take ownership over what they're doing. That's how I've always been, even when I worked for other people. I didn't see myself as just an employee. I was building something, protecting it, making it better.

I divide people into two mentalities: hourly versus owner. And listen, you can be an employee and still think like an owner. It's about mentality, not your job title. Those are the people I want in my corner because, when the pressure's on—and in hospitality, it's always on—they're the ones who aren't just looking at the clock, waiting for their shift to be over. They're looking at the guest.

One of the biggest mistakes I've made—and I'll admit this openly—is not always seeing the talent right in front of me. You've got people who've been with you for years, doing a great job day in and day out, and after a while you take it for granted. You start to see their work as a given. But here's the truth: People need to hear it. They need to know you see them, that you recognize they're doing a great job, not just at their specific tasks, but on a concept level.

The only way you grow is by elevating people. I want my team to be more than just employees. I want them to think like entrepreneurs, to be invested in the spaces we run as if they were their own.

One of the best tools we've put in place that I think really makes people feel like they're part of something bigger is biannual reviews. Twice a year, every single person gets a one-on-one sit-down. Good, bad, indifferent—we lay it all out. People love it. They want to know where they stand. They want to hear what they're doing well and what needs work.

It's not just about giving direction; it's about showing them you're paying attention. Nobody wants to feel invisible, especially when they're putting in the work. And we don't yell. That's a big one for me. I don't think you get great hospitality through fear. You get it through culture. Through accountability. Through shared standards. If I'm walking the floor and I correct someone, it's not to embarrass them. It's to raise the bar. Every guest, every shift, every touchpoint—it all adds up.

Something everyone on my team—from the bussers to the social media managers—knows is that when you come to work, you leave your bad weather behind. I don't care what happened in your day—your fight with your roommate, your broken-down car, the fact that your landlord's a pain—that stays outside. Inside, we're on stage. We're creating a party, we're creating an experience. People aren't just coming in for a drink or a steak; they're coming in to feel something. If you can't bring the smile, the energy, and the focus, you're in the wrong place.

That's not just about guest service. It's about consistency. Guests don't come back because we nailed it one night; they come back because they know they're going to feel that same energy every time. And that only happens when the team feels ownership, when they're not just clocking in but taking it personally.

I think about leading a team in terms of the emotional bank account. You can't just be in the red all the time. You can't only go to someone when they've screwed up. If you do that, they'll start to tune you out. You've got to be in the black, too—praising them when they nail it, thanking them for going the extra mile.

I'll admit, when things are busy, I have to push myself to do this. In the middle of a huge event or when I'm juggling five things at once, it's easy to forget to say the good things. But if you want people to stick with you, you've got to balance it out.

I've seen how powerful those deposits can be. I've had people tell me years later about one compliment I gave them in passing— something I don't even remember saying—and how it stuck with them. That's humbling. And it's also a reminder that you never know which moment is going to be the one that keeps someone going when they're tired or doubting themselves.

The other side of that coin is the withdrawals—the times you have to call someone out. And believe me, those are necessary, too. If someone's dragging the team down, if they're cutting corners, you can't ignore it. But if all you ever do is withdraw, that account hits zero real fast, and you're not getting that person's best anymore.

Trust is the foundation of any team. And when that trust gets broken? There's nothing worse. We've seen everything you can imagine— people trying to skim money, comping meals for friends, even bringing their own product into the restaurant to give away. One time, at one of my restaurants, we had a chef bring in his own fish so he could send sushi out to friends and family for free. Can you imagine? This guy was sourcing his own seafood, smuggling it into the restaurant every night, and pushing out double the amount of sashimi, all to give his friends a free dinner. You track everything in this business, so when something doesn't add up, I find it.

That was not a pretty conversation.

Theft is bad enough, but in hospitality, it's also personal. We're all working our asses off to make this thing run, and then someone decides to take advantage? You already know: I take it personal.

The trust goes both ways—I have to trust my team, and they have to trust me, which means I always have to protect them. One thing I'll never tolerate is a guest mistreating my team. I don't care who they are, how much they're spending, or who their dad is. You treat my people like shit, you're gone.

I've had servers come to the back in tears because some entitled guest crossed the line. When that happens, my priority is my team, not the sale. We remove the guest, period. And honestly? I never regret it. I will personally walk over to that table and make sure you know exactly why you're being shown the door. I'm an animal about this. No one's going to be disrespectful to my people in my place and get away with it.

That's not just about being the person in charge—it's about setting the tone. When your team knows you'll go to bat for them, they'll go to bat for you. If you want to last in this business, and if you want to build a team that will go the distance, you have to be thinking about the long game with your people, too. You can't think of them as bodies filling a shift; they're the face of your brand.

That's why I try to promote from within whenever I can. There's nothing more powerful than showing someone that they can move up here. I've taken hourly team members and career-pathed them into management roles, and I'll tell you, that's one of the most satisfying parts of my job. When people feel like they can grow, they stay. When they feel stuck, they're gone. It's that simple.

The truth is, career growth in hospitality isn't just about titles. It's about responsibility. I can call you a manager all day long, but if you're not making decisions, if you're not trusted with the business, it doesn't mean anything. Ownership—even in small doses—changes how people work. It makes them sharper, more invested, and more protective of the guest experience.

The biggest key to a strong team is the leadership. And the best superpower for a leader is knowing how to do every single job in the building and being willing to do it. That's what earns you respect. That's what makes your team take you seriously. And that's how I built my career. To be a satellite owner doesn't work. Your team needs to see your face and hear your words. You can't trust somebody else to report on how things are going, because the financials could be perfectly fine while, visibly, the place is not. Once that turns, it turns so fast it's hard to get it back. Presence matters in this business more than almost any other.

I've been a bartender. I've managed the floor. I've opened and closed. I've cleaned up puke in the bathroom at 3:00 a.m., stacked glasses till my arms were sore, done the inventory, jumped behind the bar during a rush. There's not a job in this business I haven't done, and my team knows it.

That's the part I love most. No one at my venues—no bartender, no server, no dishwasher—can ever come to me and say, "If you don't do this, I'm walking." Why? Because they know I'll do it my fucking self—yes, I wouldn't hesitate to start running drinks if I had to, and everyone who works with me knows that. That's the kind of culture I think makes for long-term success.

I walk into my venues and I don't sit down in an office or hang out at the bar like I'm some big shot. I walk the floor. I pick up trash. Constantly. I want my people to see me doing it. I want them to see me wiping down tables, picking up a napkin someone dropped, walking a guest to the bathroom. Culture in hospitality isn't a mission statement on a website. It's the way you look someone in the eye when they walk in, the way you deal with them when there's a problem, the way you close the night. That can't happen without a team I trust.

CHAPTER EIGHT

YOUR NAME IS EVERYTHING: LESSONS IN INTELLECTUAL PROPERTY

I'm a hospitality guy. My passion is curating experiences, mostly through clubs and restaurants and hotels, and thinking about ways to take hospitality to the next level. Over the last several decades, I also have found myself thinking a lot about more traditional business concepts, and one of the most important concepts is intellectual property (IP). I've been lucky to have some great mentors and friends to help me along the way, but I've also learned a lot by doing. Transitioning from "I run one club" to "I run several clubs and a restaurant" to "I run a large-scale hospitality group" isn't something that happens overnight; but if you're starting a business, you need to be thinking about how you'll handle its growth.

Let me say this loud and clear from the jump: One of the most important pieces of owning a business is intellectual property. Period. It doesn't matter if you're opening a boutique hotel in South Beach or launching a vegan pet food line or selling arancini based on your nonna's recipe from the old country out of a food truck—if you're not thinking about your IP, you're leaving money, control, and a whole lot of future leverage on the table.

When people start throwing around the term "intellectual property," they usually mean the big four: patents, copyrights, trademarks, and trade secrets.

Let's start with patents. A patent is basically a government-issued permission slip that says, "You, and only you, can make, sell, or use this thing for a set number of years." That "thing" could be an invention, a process, a piece of technology—anything new, useful, and not obvious. In hospitality, maybe it's a piece of kitchen equipment you designed to speed up service or a unique cocktail smoking device that wows guests at the bar. You get twenty years of exclusivity from the filing date, which buys you time to capitalize on your idea before the copycats show up.

Now, copyrights are a whole different animal. Copyright protects creative work—menus, interior design elements, photography, video, even the written descriptions on your website. Remember: You can't copyright ideas—only the expression of an idea. So you can't copyright "a tropical-themed restaurant," but you can copyright the exact menu descriptions, the original cocktail recipes as written, and the photography you shot for promotion.

Trademarks are your brand's calling card. They cover your name, logo, slogan, or even your unique décor style if it's distinctive enough. Think of the LIV logo in Miami nightlife—you see it on a flyer, and you know exactly the kind of night you're in for. Trademarks are powerful because they can last forever if you keep using and renewing them. They're also one of the fastest ways to build serious brand value, because guests associate them directly with the experience you deliver.

And then there are trade secrets—the guarded, behind-the-scenes stuff that gives your business its edge. Maybe it's your restaurant's signature sauce recipe. You don't register a trade secret—you protect it by keeping it under wraps. The moment it's public, it's gone. That's why some food and beverage companies keep their recipes locked in safes or limit kitchen prep knowledge to just one or two trusted staff members.

Here's the thing: Protecting your IP in hospitality isn't about being paranoid; it's about being smart. We all work too hard to create something unique just to let someone else swoop in and duplicate it. Whether it's the vibe in your nightclub, the look of your menu, the logo on your merch, or the process you use to deliver an unforgettable guest experience, you've got to know which IP tool fits the job. In this business, once your ideas are out there, they spread fast—and it's a lot easier to defend them if you've set up protection from day one.

If you're building something you actually care about, something that could grow, scale, sell, or even just survive past its first couple years, IP is the foundation you can't build without. It's what lets you build a brand, not just a one-off. And yet, I see people making mistakes with this all the time—even smart, successful people who should know better. When we go to open a restaurant, the first thing we do is make a list of potential names and google them.

Why do we do that? We want to see if there's another Komodo, if there's another Papi Steak, if there's another LIV, because you can't get an IP, a trademark, a copyright on a name that's already been taken. When you're starting a project, no matter the scale, you have to envision a future in which it has grown into something bigger than you can imagine right now and take the steps to protect it accordingly. It's not about being cocky and saying, "Oh, I'm going to open this restaurant that will immediately become a huge hit and have locations all around the world in the next eighteen months," though if you want to put that on your vision board, go ahead. It's about acknowledging that your time and resources are valuable, and you owe it to yourself to protect them.

When it comes to IP, I always advise people to hire an attorney. You do your own due diligence, too, but this is not an area that you should skimp on. You and your attorney will need to do proper trademark searches, check domain availability, look at social media handles, and understand the competitive landscape in your industry.

This might seem tedious, but it's absolutely critical. I've seen too many businesses that had to rebrand entirely because they didn't do this homework up front. You think you created a product that's crushing it, it's amazing, it's gonna be huge—guess what? There's one in London and now they're suing you and now they own your business. Is it worth it? No.

Imagine building a brand for years, getting people to know your name, building reputation and loyalty, and then having to throw it all away because someone else owned the rights.

Let me give you a real example that perfectly illustrates this point. A few months ago, I was on the phone with someone I've known for years. He reached out to say he'd just opened a steakhouse, and he called it Prime. It's doing really well. He was excited, wanted to hop on a call to chat about it, maybe even get some advice.

I texted him back and said, "That's great. I'd love to talk and help in any way I can. But first thing—just gotta say this straight up: You called it Prime . . . and there's no way you're ever going to trademark that name."

Prime is not a bad name, but it's not unique. It's not protectable. It's everywhere. Just in Miami, we've got five different restaurants with "Prime" in the name—all successful, all already staked out in the steak-and-seafood space. Even if my friend's Prime is crushing it in Atlanta, he's boxed in now. There's no path for expansion under that name. No ability to sell the brand later. No legal recourse if someone in another state starts calling their steak-and-seafood spot Prime, too. It's a mistake, plain and simple.

Now, look, I get the impulse. "Prime" sounds strong, sexy, high-end. But that's exactly the problem. A lot of people have already thought the same thing. So when I'm opening a new restaurant or venue, I make sure the name is unique, something I can own, something I can take national, global even. I'm not interested in just opening one place. I'm building brands. A brand without protectable IP? It's like building a house on someone else's land.

So here's Rule #1: Do your damn IP check. Before you launch anything. Doesn't matter how obscure the name seems. Even if there's a tiny bistro using the name in some little town in the Alps you've never heard of, it still matters. Because the second you hit it big, someone's going to come out of the woodwork with a claim. Or worse—you'll find out too late that you can't scale. And trust me, if you want to grow your brand or sell it someday, you don't want any obstacles in your way.

Why am I devoting a whole chapter in my book to IP? Because to me, IP is everything as an entrepreneur. When you own your IP, that's what allows you to make decisions later. It's your name, your brand, your concept that you own. And there's so many things that go into that. I never go into a project thinking it's going to be a one-off. I'm growing brands, and I can't do that if my IP isn't locked up.

For me, at this stage in my career, I always have to have an IP ownership stake. A lot of very successful businesses have said, "Hey, will you partner with me in Miami?" And I say no unless I can be a partner in the IP, because I feel like IP is the most valuable part of the business. If you can't sell that IP, if you can't grow that IP, and if you don't have ownership in the IP, then you're really just an employee. I've been an employee, and I learned a lot doing it, but at this point in my career, I'm not interested in doing work for hire. I want to feel like I have a role in shaping projects not just as they launch but as they evolve.

Taking care of your IP is the homework of any entrepreneur. I take it a lot more seriously than I ever took any of my actual homework in school. So when we go to find a name for one of our restaurants, or if you're building a nightclub or a consumer brand, you need to be able to name it and then protect that name. If you're launching a product and it involves something you've invented, the patent process is a key part of IP. Everything you do is in some way your IP, and you need to be thinking about how to use it and how to protect it.

Now, sometimes you can't entirely own the IP yourself. That happens. And in those cases, you need to make sure the deal is still right for you.

Take LIV, for example. That was one of my first big nightlife hits. My partner on that is Jeffrey Soffer, who owns the Fontainebleau Hotel—and by extension, he owns the IP for LIV. But in our agreement, we put it in writing that he can't open another LIV without me, and I can't open another LIV without him. That way, I'm protected. We're locked in together, and nobody can run off with the brand behind the other's back. I also know that if there's ever an instance in which I have to protect the LIV brand, I'm not going to be doing it on my own, because he's part of it, too.

But there are also times when I got it wrong. When I went to raise the $10 million I needed to open my restaurant Komodo, I had this big, exciting vision. I'm pitching people. I'm telling them, "Not only are you investing in this restaurant, but you're also getting the IP." That was the hook. At the time, I thought that was smart, generous even. I would get the money I needed, and my investors would feel like they were part of the project beyond just writing checks.

But here's what actually happened.

Komodo did so well that, of course, I go and open another Komodo in Dallas. It's another market, completely different from Miami and requiring me to do a lot of work taking our existing DNA and translating it for a new city. It's a whole new build-out, new staff, new P&L, new everything. And guess what? Those original investors now come along for a free ride. They've already made their money back on the first location, and now they're automatically getting equity in a second one—even though they didn't lift a finger, didn't write another check, didn't take on any of the risk that comes with opening a second spot. If I open more Komodos (and I almost certainly will), those original investors will continue to hold equity in the brand even though I'm the one actually building it. It's a real miss on my part. What I did, without realizing it, was tie up the IP to the original restaurant in a way that would keep me locked in every time I expanded. And let's be real, when you're building a brand like Komodo, it's not supposed to be just one restaurant. It's supposed to be a platform—a concept that travels. It's on me for not seeing that from the get-go—that this was going to be a concept that would travel to other locations, which it has. Now we have Komodo in Las Vegas, and I'm looking at new cities, too.

The lesson? Be specific. Be careful. Don't just offer someone IP to make a deal sound better. You need to know what you're offering, and how it'll impact you not just today but five years from now when you're scaling. If you're not clear and precise from the beginning, you'll be the one paying for it later.

One of the biggest things I hope you take from this book is that you should always, always think long-term. Think about where this thing could go—five years, ten years, maybe more. Is it expandable? Is it sellable? Can you license it? Can you defend it in court?

The truth is, IP is leverage. It's power. It's the thing that lets you call the shots later on.

A lot of people want to partner with me, and I get it. I've built a reputation here, and people know a new David Grutman restaurant in Miami is always going to get attention. They also know I'm meticulous, and any project I'm involved in is going to be done really well. I'd want to partner with me, too! I know my personal brand is attractive to people because there's a dedicated community that comes with it. But unless I'm going to own a piece of the IP, I'm not even picking up the phone.

There are different ways to do it, too. Management contracts, for example, have allowed me to leverage other people's money to build my own intellectual property. If you've ever been to a restaurant inside a hotel or casino, it's probably been a management contract deal. Essentially, I could put my brand, my concepts, and my operational expertise into a property without having to fund the build-out myself. In places like Las Vegas, nearly 99 percent of restaurants operate this way. With a management contract, I will take a percentage of the gross revenue and receive an incentive bonus on profits. It wasn't as lucrative as a lease deal, but it does mitigate some of the financial risk. At the same time, your name is still on the door, so the risk to your reputation is the same as if you were putting the money up yourself. You're still invested.

With a management deal, from day one, I can generate cash flow. Unlike traditional investments, where you spend years paying back capital, management contracts allow me to start earning immediately while simultaneously building my brand's presence and credibility. Owning the intellectual property means that every successful location strengthened the brand for future opportunities. If people love your restaurant in Las Vegas, say, they'll want to come to a place you might be opening closer to where they live. Those deals have added tangible value because it demonstrates cash flow to potential partners and investors.

Without ownership, you're building someone else's equity, not yours. For me, that's a deal-breaker. I've learned that every project I take on has to fit into the larger strategy. I'm not just looking for a quick win—I'm looking for things that can scale, that add to the portfolio, that strengthen the foundation I've already built. If I say yes to a deal, I'm tying up time, resources, and my own reputation, and that's a commitment I don't take lightly. And when the time comes to package or sell part of the company, if I don't own what I've built, it doesn't have value.

I'm always thinking about this. Pharrell and I had a conversation recently. He came to me with an idea: LV Lovers Bars—a kind of nightlife extension for Louis Vuitton. I could see it in my mind immediately, because his vision is so exacting and we work so well together. But Louis Vuitton is a big company, and I had an important question: "Are they going to give us a piece of the IP?"

He laughed and said, "Louis Vuitton is never going to give you a piece of any IP. But it will be a really great thing for you to be able to say that you worked with Louis Vuitton."

I saw the vision: Louis Vuitton is one of the most recognizable luxury brands in the world, and people would go nuts for a physical space that wasn't a store. It would make money, it would generate buzz, it would be an amazing vehicle to launch other opportunities.

But you know what I said? No. Not without the IP.

Look, I love Louis Vuitton. It's an amazing brand. But I'm not here for resume bullet points. I'm not here to be a hired gun, just making other people richer and not having any true say in the biggest decisions. If I'm going to put my energy, creativity, and time into something, then I need to own a piece of it. Otherwise, I'm not fulfilled. I'm not proud. And I'm not building anything that lasts.

So now anything that we do, we own the IP, no matter what. This has become nonnegotiable for me.

Now, there are times when it makes sense to share IP. But only when the other person brings real value to the table, not just money. A great example of this is Pharrell himself. He and I co-own the IP for the hotel and restaurants we did together. That's because we built those things together—from concept to execution. They were joint ventures right from the jump. He's not just some face slapped on a brand. He's actively involved. He brings vision, credibility, style—he's now the men's creative director at Louis Vuitton. The man's got serious equity in the culture. So in that case, sharing IP made perfect sense.

And the value that a partner brings to the table can look like a lot of different things. I've been friends for a long time with a guy named David Einhorn. Everyone calls him "Papi," and anytime we'd hang out in Miami, I knew we'd be in my backyard grilling—Papi has the magic touch when it comes to steak. One night, Papi was just out there grilling, doing his Papi thing. He had this whole vibe about the way he cooked: the energy, the confidence. He kept saying, "We gotta put Papi Steak on the menu at Komodo."

And I was like, you know what? Let's do it. So we did: a Kosher steak with his special "Papi sauce." It took off. People were obsessed with this steak, and it became a thing to get a reservation at Komodo and treat your friends to the Papi steak. So that backyard idea turned into something way bigger than either of us expected. We thought, why not open a whole restaurant around this? That's when the idea for Papi Steak was born.

We decided to look for a second-generation restaurant, which basically meant a place that had opened before but failed. The appeal of this was that the kitchen, bar, bathrooms, and HVAC were already in place. So instead of starting from scratch—which for a first-generation restaurant could cost anywhere from $10 to $30 million and take years to develop—we only had to invest about $1.4 million to get it up and running.

The spot we found was in the South of Fifth district in South Beach, a buzzing new culinary area in Miami. It was smaller than what I was used to—just 93 seats, compared to the 200- to 500-seat restaurants I normally opened, but I knew a more intimate space would make guests feel like they were coming to an over-the-top dinner party hosted by a pair of friends.

When it came time to pick a name for the restaurant, there was really only one choice: Papi Steak, after our star menu item. We also serve dishes like wagyu pastrami and truffle chicken, and there's always a pretty good chance Papi himself will swing by your table to greet you just as enthusiastically as he would if we were still grilling in my backyard. Basically, everything at Papi Steak is designed to make people talk and to come back for more.

It was important to me to go fifty-fifty on the IP with Papi. It was his first foray into restaurants, with me bringing a lot of the experience and institutional knowledge; but it was his steak that made the whole thing possible. Papi is also a showman, and it was easy to see how that talent would be an important part of the restaurant. Plus, he's a good friend and someone I was genuinely excited about going into business with.

I call it a mitzvah relationship. It was a mitzvah that he got a steakhouse, sure—but honestly, it was a mitzvah for me, too. I got to work with someone who's not just talented but driven and full of heart. And those kinds of relationships? You don't manufacture them. They either happen or they don't. Papi works as hard as I do on the restaurant—he's in there at dinnertime six nights a week, touching tables and taking pictures with people who know him from social media.

Now, six years later, we've both made millions because of that one backyard moment. And it's not just the money—it's the growth. Remember, I'm a long-ball guy. I saw something in Papi—his talent, his energy, his instinct—and I didn't just want to capitalize on it for one thing. I wanted to build with him. How do we grow that talent? How do we make it last? That's the mindset I've always had. It doesn't happen overnight.

And here we are, six years in. We just opened Papi Steak Las Vegas in December 2023. And that's a whole new level. Vegas is no joke—it's one of the most competitive hospitality markets in the world—but we brought the full Miami energy to the Fontainebleau Las Vegas. We knew people wanted more than just a meal. They wanted to feel something. And that's what Papi Steak delivers every time: this electric mix of luxury, spectacle, and straight-up great food. We signed a contract that will have us opening in Dubai, and I'm certain more will follow because we've succeeded at creating a brand that really feels special to our guests.

What I love about my relationship with Papi is that it started pure. It wasn't some corporate thing. It was friends grilling in my backyard. And now, he knows as much about the restaurant business as I do. He's seen it all—kitchens, service, branding, staffing. He's not just a guy with a good idea anymore. He's a true partner, and I'm proud to own something with him.

* * *

Another big trap people fall into is naming things after themselves. You might think it's smart branding—putting your name on the door. Makes it personal. Makes it yours. But in reality? It's risky.

Look at John Varvatos or, honestly, a ton of other fashion designers and entrepreneurs. A lot of them don't even own their names anymore. They sold their brand and, with it, the rights to use their own name. And now? That name is out in the world, being used on products or in ways they might not even agree with.

And let's be honest, what happens if the business fails? You really want your name attached to something that flopped? Remember Winker's Diner? It was named after one of my cats. It didn't work out, and for months I couldn't even look at the poor guy. That's what happens when you tie your identity too closely to a brand. You lose objectivity. And you lose options.

If I had launched a skincare line and called it "David Grutman Beauty" instead of creating a distinct brand name, and then I sold that company, I wouldn't even be able to use David Grutman for future ventures. Think about that—you could literally sell away your own identity. Someone could be out here slapping "David Grutman" on T-shirts and there wouldn't be a thing I could do about it.

When I sold 51 percent of my company, they weren't cutting me a check for brands I didn't own the intellectual property for. That's not how real deals work. Nobody's handing you millions just because you've got a cool spot on the corner or a line out the door.

They're buying because they see runway. They believe they can take what you've built, pour gas on the fire, and turn it into something much bigger.

If you don't own your IP, that runway disappears. Without it, they can't scale it, can't drop it into new markets, can't build it into a powerhouse. They're not buying your "vibe" or your "concept"—they're buying the rights. If you don't have the rights, you've got nothing to sell except one location's worth of cash flow.

IP is leverage. IP that is protected can be replicated, licensed, franchised, and scaled until it's in every market your buyer can dream of. That's what gets the big checks signed.

Here's the thing most people never figure out: The real, life-changing money isn't in staying hyper-focused on what happens tonight. Yeah, you can live well, pay yourself, make some profit. But what about tomorrow? What about next year or ten years from now? That's why the game-changer is the exit. That's when all those years of late nights, stress, and building finally translate into a serious payday.

So sharing IP can absolutely be the way to go; you just need to be extremely thoughtful about when and how you do it.

With Papi Steak and David Einhorn, sharing that IP made complete sense. He wasn't just a silent investor or someone providing capital. He was the heart of what made that concept special. He was as committed to the success of that brand as I was. In that case, sharing IP created alignment and ensured we were both fully invested in making it work.

But contrast that with the typical scenario where someone approaches you and says, "I have a great location, you have a great concept, let's partner up." If they're just providing real estate or capital—and you're providing the concept, the operations, the brand, the marketing—why should they own any of the IP? They'll get their return on their real estate or their capital investment. The IP should stay with whoever created and is building the brand.

Looking back, my relationship with IP has evolved significantly. In the early days with LIV, I was just excited to be in business. I was thinking about cash flow, about creating something cool, about building my reputation. I wasn't thinking strategically about asset creation and long-term value building.

But as I've built more businesses and seen more deals, I've realized that IP is often the most valuable asset you create. It's more valuable than your physical locations, your equipment, your inventory. It's the thing that can be scaled infinitely without additional physical investment.

This realization changed how I approach every new venture. Now, when I'm thinking about a new business idea or partnership venture, I'm thinking about the IP strategy. What are we going to call this? Who's going to own it? How do we protect it? How do we structure it so that it can grow beyond what we're building today?

This might seem rigid, but it's actually liberating. It helps me focus on the opportunities that are truly aligned with my long-term strategy rather than getting distracted by deals that might look good in the short term but don't build lasting value.

To me, business is about creating something that can outlast you, that can grow beyond what you originally envisioned, that can become valuable to other people who might want to acquire it or partner with it.

Your IP is what makes that possible. It's what transforms a single location or single product into a brand. It's what allows you to scale without being physically present in every location. It's what creates the foundation for licensing deals, franchising opportunities, acquisition offers, and all the other ways that businesses grow and create value over time.

So, yes, dealing with IP is the boring homework of being an entrepreneur. It's not as fun as designing your space or creating your menu or launching your marketing campaign. But it's the foundation that makes everything else possible.

And here's the thing—if you get it right from the beginning, you never have to think about it again. You can focus on building your business knowing that you own what you're creating. But if you get it wrong, it can haunt you for years. You'll find yourself in situations where you've built something valuable, but you don't fully own it, or where you want to expand, but you can't because someone else controls the name.

Take my advice: Do the boring work up front. Protect your IP. Own your name. Everything else you want to accomplish as an entrepreneur depends on it. At the end of the day, your name—your brand, your concept, your IP—that's everything. It's what allows you to make decisions later. It's what gives you the freedom to grow, to pivot, to sell, to scale. It's the difference between building a job for yourself and building an asset that can create wealth and opportunities for years to come.

Don't make the mistakes I made. Learn from them. Own your IP, protect it fiercely, and only share it with people who are truly building something with you for the long haul. Everything else in your business will flow from getting this foundation right.

CHAPTER NINE

EXIT STRATEGIES

In 2018, I founded Groot Hospitality (notice that it's called "Groot" as in "Grutman," but it's not called "David Grutman Hospitality," because I take my own advice!) to serve as both the foundation and the umbrella for my clubs, restaurants, and future properties. Less than two years later, I sold a 51 percent stake in Groot to Live Nation, one of the biggest events and entertainment companies on the planet.

Selling all or part of a company is one of the most misunderstood concepts in business, especially in hospitality-based businesses. When people talk about an "exit" in business, they're usually referring to the moment when a founder or investor cashes out of a company. It's the end of one chapter and, ideally, the beginning of something new—whether that's retirement, another venture, or just a really long vacation. But for all the hype around exits, especially in startup and investment circles, I think it's worth unpacking what an exit actually means, because it's not just a finish line; it's a strategy, a mindset, and sometimes a surprise twist.

For some people, an exit is when you stop being actively involved in the business you helped build. That could mean selling the whole company to another group, merging with someone bigger, or stepping back and letting others run it while you collect a check. Sometimes it's a full buyout where you're completely done, and other times it's partial—you sell off a significant piece, maybe give up control, but you're still around in some way. For others, an exit isn't so much an exit as it is bringing on a partner who will help you turn a business that's successful now into a business that will continue to thrive a hundred years down the line. It requires some imagination and some trust in what you've built. If half of the billion-dollar business you could have with the right partner is more valuable than what you have right now, you owe it to yourself to really think about it.

People assume exits are always these grand, champagne-popping moments. And, yes, sometimes they are. But more often, they're messy. They take time. You're negotiating valuations, dealing with lawyers, managing employees' emotions, and continuing to operate the business as it is while also planning your next steps. It can feel like you're living a double life.

There's a big difference, too, between different types of exits. If you're a founder, your exit might be selling the company you built from the ground up. Maybe it's a private sale to a strategic buyer—someone who wants your product or market position. Or maybe it's a private equity firm that sees potential and wants to scale it.

Or maybe you go public, which is another kind of exit, though that comes with its own set of rules and headaches.

If you're an investor, you might be looking to exit your position when the company raises a new round of funding or sells. In those cases, you've put money in, helped grow the business, and now you're looking to turn that investment into a return. That could be two times your money or twenty times, depending on the deal.

But the word "exit" can be misleading, because you don't always leave with everything you hoped for. Sometimes you exit early because you have to—things didn't go the way you planned, and getting out with something is better than going down with the ship. Other times you might feel like you sold too soon, or maybe you stayed in too long. Timing is everything, but timing is also impossible to perfect. You make the best call you can, based on the information you've got and what your gut is telling you.

An exit isn't just about money. Yes, it's great if you walk away with a big payout, but I've seen exits that were emotionally taxing, and I've seen exits bring people a massive sense of relief. So part of defining an exit, at least for me, is being honest with yourself about what success looks like. Is it a certain dollar amount? Is it freeing up your time? Is it knowing the business is in good hands?

I also think more people should talk about life after the exit. It's not always as glamorous as it sounds. You've got more money in the bank, but now what? What you're also getting, if you're bringing on a partner the way I did, is the access to capital to grow your brand, and that means you have to be actively working toward that growth. If you don't have an idea about what's next, that can be unsettling. So a big part of defining your exit should include thinking about what you want after the deal closes.

At the end of the day, an exit is a milestone, not the end of the road. It's a reflection of the work you've put in and a stepping stone to whatever comes next. And if you've played your cards right, it's not just an ending—it's a beginning. Because here's the thing about bringing in an equity partner: It gives you more infrastructure, more deal flow, and a line of credit to tap into, because that's what holds a lot of us up—just money. So many times, especially in hospitality, I've seen people relying on money to come in to fund the next thing. No money, no next thing. You're always waiting for money to come in so that you can turn to the next thing, and that can keep you from breaking through the next ceiling. An exit, if done right, provides you with resources that accelerate your ability to grow your business.

Generations ago, whether you owned a restaurant or a club, you followed a pretty standard playbook. You'd open a restaurant—say it was wildly successful—and you'd ride it out for as long as you could in your specific market. Maybe, just maybe, you'd get a call from Vegas and open a second location. A third if you got lucky—maybe in Miami. And that was it. That was the extent of the empire.

The people who would do this would make a decent chunk of money. Some of them bought real estate with it, and some of them? They blew it—drugs, girls, the usual distractions. And eventually the brand would die, and with it, the legacy they could've built. Instead, signs come down and new signs go up. As someone who has lived in Miami for most of his adult life, I'm constantly seeing restaurants and clubs open in spaces that used to be other restaurants and clubs.

Looking back, I can see exactly where they went wrong. People working in this industry in the '90s and the early '00s, when I got to Miami, were thinking like operators, not builders. They were focused on the day-to-day grind of keeping a single location performing well, perfecting their craft, maybe becoming legends in their own market. But they never stepped back and asked the bigger question: What if this could be something more?

They didn't think about systems. They didn't think about replication. They didn't think about what would happen to their legacy when they weren't there to personally oversee every detail. And most importantly, they didn't think about building something that could outlive them.

My generation figured out a different model. A smarter model. We learned how to take a brand and build a real company around it, not just a mom-and-pop operation with a name you'd recognize if you were a local but something with real infrastructure. Something corporate, something that could scale. Something that wasn't just a one-off but instead part of a larger story, because that's how I think about my business. My brand is something that people all over the world feel connected to, and it's how I keep those connections strong that makes me stand out.

It wasn't just about having a good product anymore. It was about having a good business. And knowing the difference between those two things is one of the most important discernments a founder can ever make.

There's a difference between opening new spots or launching new products and being truly scalable. In hospitality, a product might be a great restaurant with the best barbecue in town. Reservations are booked months in advance, there's always a line for walk-ins, and the local news frequently stops by to do human-interest stories on the pulled pork made with someone's grandma's secret recipe. There's absolutely nothing wrong with having a product. In fact, to become a successful business, the product has to be good—no one's going to want to invest in a second location unless the first is knocking it out of the park. But to truly scale, you need systems. You need to think about how to replicate the experience without being in the room every night. In hospitality, that can be tough because so much of the work is curating the vibe and making sure the experience is on point. Becoming a company means operations, supply chain, tech support, logistics—the unsexy stuff that turns a one-hit wonder into a business. Then there's marketing. You can't just rely on word of mouth forever. You've got to figure out how to tell your story to more people in more places without losing what made it special in the first place. Those are the things you want to nail before you even think about exiting—your company has to be in order for potential investors and partners to take you seriously.

Recognizing and understanding that shift was massive for me. I started seeing my peers make exits, and it opened my eyes to what was possible. The Light Group, which operates a number of huge restaurants, was acquired by a larger company in 2014. Noah Tepperberg and the Tao Group sold to Madison Square Garden Entertainment. Around this time, I sold my pre–Groot Hospitality management company to a company called SFX Entertainment, who were making moves in the world of electronic music, buying up festivals, and investing in nightlife spots all over the world. It's a long and not that interesting story, but SFX eventually went bankrupt. It could have been a disaster for me, but it proved to be the opposite. Amid the chaos, I got my company back. And that was actually a blessing because that's when I started diversifying– adding restaurants, cultural projects, moving into new markets. I realized we weren't just in the nightlife game anymore. We were in the business business.

And let me tell you, when you start thinking in terms of multiples, it changes the whole equation. We weren't thinking, "Can this make $2 million this year?" We were thinking, "Can we build something that someone will pay $200 million for?"

This shift in thinking was groundbreaking. Suddenly, corporations started saying, hey, the hospitality business is a good business. The math was simple, but it was profound. Instead of just making a small amount of money each year from steady operations, we structured things so that we could benefit from earnouts–performance-based payouts that rewarded us for hitting certain targets. But it wasn't just about the volume of check sales anymore. I wasn't deriving my value solely from how much money we made on any given night. The real shift was that we were also getting compensated based on the value of the brand we had built. That meant the stronger our brand became in the market—through recognition, guest loyalty, and overall influence—the more valuable our earnouts became. It turned short-term revenue into long-term brand equity. To gain that kind of wealth was a game-changer. It's one thing to get a couple million, but to get $30 million or $50 million or $100 million or $200 million—that's a real amount of money that you can take and do other things with. That's generational money. That's change-your-life money. For me, that money allowed me to look at everything I'd accomplished and say: What's next?

If "what's next?" is a question that keeps popping up for you, it might be a sign that you're ready to bring on a partner who can help you reach that next level. A lot of people ask me not just how I knew I was ready, but how I knew Michael Rapino and Live Nation were the right partners for me.

My answer: Live Nation is at the apex of all things hospitality and entertainment. Knowing that, I built a business and a brand that they actively wanted to be involved with. The brand was strong. The numbers spoke for themselves. I always knew that I was building something people would want and that I would be viewed as a potential purchase or partnership. It was important to me to structure my business as a real company, with a full C-suite of experts and solid contracts and clear, easy-to-understand financials. It's easy, in hospitality, to find yourself doing math on the backs of cocktail napkins, to sign deals over drinks instead of in conference rooms. It was important to me, as I continued to expand Groot, to be not only successful but professional, and I think that's something people took note of. When Michael Rapino came to me about becoming my partner, I was ready, and he changed my life.

Live Nation owns 51 percent of Groot Hospitality now—a majority stake, with me still a huge part of operations and decision-making. Here's the thing about deciding what percentage to sell: It's not just about the money. It's about what you need personally, what the business needs to grow, and what kind of partnership you want. Over the years, I've had the opportunity to sell more of my shares, and there will probably be a time when I make that choice; but now, with so many exciting projects on the horizon, it's important to both me and to Michael Rapino that I continue to have a meaningful stake in the company. When it comes to determining how much (or how little) equity to sell, I've seen people miss it both ways. I've seen people wait too long and miss the boat, finding themselves priced too high for anyone to want to make a serious offer. I've also seen people sell too early, and now they find themselves turning over 75 percent of profits to a partner who isn't really bringing a lot of value.

Michael didn't just come in with a check. He came in with vision. He said, "We see what you're doing, and we want to help you take it global."

And listen, choosing a partner is like getting married. Don't just take the biggest ring. Take the one who's going to stick with you when things go to shit.

The courtship process is important, too. You need to understand their culture, their decision-making process, their long-term vision. Do they see you as just another acquisition, or do they see you as a strategic partner? Are they going to let you keep doing what you do best, or are they going to try to change everything? By the time I sold, Groot Hospitality was functioning like a well-oiled machine. We had a corporate structure where department heads would handle everything from marketing to operations to sales. We were overseeing our existing venues and developing concepts and partnerships for new ones, proving concepts in Miami and then taking them to other cities where we knew our core demographic would follow.

I spent a lot of time with the Live Nation team before we made the deal. I met with Michael multiple times. I understood how he operated, what he valued, what his track record was with other partnerships. I wasn't just selling to a company; I was choosing to work with them. Because guess what? They did exactly what I hoped they would do when things got tough.

I sold in October 2019. In March 2020, the world shut down. No shows. No travel. No nightlife. That could have been a disaster. And honestly, if I had been dealing with a different kind of partner, it might have been. But Michael? He didn't flinch. He didn't pull the plug. He said, "What do you need? What can I do for you? How can I help?"

I think it's hard to really know someone when things are always great—it's easy to be a good partner when business is booming. Michael showed me, in a difficult moment for our industry, that he was in it for the long haul.

He could have said, "Listen, we're dealing with no touring, no concerts, no festivals." The entire live entertainment industry was on pause. Live Nation had every reason to panic, every reason to start cutting costs and protecting themselves first. He did the opposite.

And I got lucky again, because Miami was able to bounce back from the initial wave of pandemic shutdowns. We have so many great venues with outdoor space, and the weather is nice, so suddenly it was the place to be—I mean, even more so than it usually is. My numbers were through the roof in an incredibly short period of time. So my earnout was way better than anyone expected. I proved to Live Nation that they had picked the right horse to bet on.

But here's the thing about that success: It wasn't just luck. It was preparation meeting opportunity. Because we had the infrastructure, because we had the systems, because we had the right partner, we were able to pivot quickly when the opportunity presented itself.

A lot of businesses didn't survive the pandemic. A lot of partnerships didn't survive the pandemic. But ours got stronger. That's when I knew I had picked the right people. That's when I knew the deal we had made wasn't just about money. It was about building something together for the long term.

Now that Miami's leveled off more, markets have shifted and people are spending less money on going out. But the foundation we built during that time, the relationship we strengthened, the systems we put in place—that's all still there.

I meet a lot of people who say they'd never want to sell their businesses, and that's fair. A true exit isn't for everyone. What I say in response, though, is that there's always an exit. If you're passing the business on to your kids? That's an exit. Planning on managing day-to-day operations yourself until you're ready to retire? Also a kind of exit. Even taking on an outside investor where you retain majority stake—that's a form of exiting because it's shifting the balance of your business in a new way.

That's why even if you don't plan to sell, build like you are. That means professionalizing everything. You need financials. You need clean books. You need reporting, HR policies, real roles and titles, a COO who can run the day-to-day, a CFO who can model out your next twenty-four months.

A lot of people, historically, got into nightlife and entertainment so that they wouldn't have to think about "boring" stuff. The goal was to find a hot DJ, set a door policy that ensured only the coolest people in town would get in, and let the chips fall where they may. They didn't have HR. They didn't have a CFO, they didn't have a

COO, they probably didn't even have a proper accounting system. I shudder when I think about how much unaccounted-for cash must have been floating around Miami bars and clubs before I came on the scene! They were flying by the seat of their pants, making it up as they went along.

If your club is thriving, and you're still the one booking the DJ, managing payroll, checking receipts, and approving every piece of creative—you're not operating a company, and when investors are looking for places to put their money and people to get into business with, they're looking for something bigger than one club.

Investors, strategic buyers, and partners want something that can run without you. That's the irony of it. You bust your ass to make your name the brand, but the moment you want to cash out, the brand has to survive without you.

I learned this lesson the hard way. In the early days, I was involved in everything. Every decision, every approval, every problem that came up—it all landed on my desk. I thought that was what being a good leader meant. I thought that was what being indispensable meant. But indispensable is actually the opposite of what you want to be if you ever want to exit. You want to be valuable, not indispensable. There's a huge difference.

So I had to learn how to step back. I had to learn how to build systems instead of just solving problems. I had to learn how to hire people who were smarter than me in their areas and then actually let them do their jobs. It was uncomfortable at first—letting go of control always is—but it was the only way to scale. I know I talked earlier about the importance of being able to do everything, and I do obviously believe that's true. But being able to do something isn't the same as needing to doing it, and part of your job as a business owner is to recognize the value and the limits of your own time. I'm not saying I always get it right. If someone on my team sends me a draft of a promotional email and I don't like the wording they used, I will go back and forth with that person until I think it feels right, even though that's probably not the best use of my time. But I hire talented, smart people, and while I 100 percent cop to driving them nuts sometimes, I also know letting them do their work means I can spend my time growing the business in ways we all benefit from.

And the beautiful thing is, once you start building like this, the business actually runs better. You're not the bottleneck anymore. Decisions get made faster. People take ownership. And you can focus on the big picture instead of getting lost in the weeds.

A simple question to ask yourself when you're considering making an exit: Why? Do you want to bring in a corporate partner so you can expand your market or your reach, or get access to research and development money and resources you wouldn't have on your own? Do you want to be a figurehead, a face of your company who makes the rounds at conferences and brand summits but doesn't really have to worry about things like tariffs and zoning ordinances? Or do you want to *exit* exit, meaning sell your company and retire? None of these answers is wrong, but it's worth thinking about because, in a lot of ways, an exit is really just a new beginning.

Take me, for example. My day-to-day since bringing on a partner changed some, but not in the way you might think. What was great about Michael was that he wanted the entrepreneur to be the entrepreneur and to continue to grow the company. He understood that he didn't buy my company to change what made it successful. He bought it to scale what was already working.

Of course, when you own your company yourself, you don't have to get buy-in from anybody. You can make decisions in real time, pivot when you need to, take risks without committee approval.

Now that I have a corporate partner involved, we do have to get buy-in with new ideas, and we have to do reporting. If I want to open a new concept, I do have to back it up beyond "I have a great idea for a new location." But they've never said no to me, which has been great. They've been supportive of every major initiative, every expansion, every risk we've wanted to take. What's more, instead of us trying to raise money for everything, now we have a line of credit, and they'll bring us opportunities that come across their desks, too.

I won't lie: This was a big adjustment for me. When you're part of a public company like Live Nation, you have to be more organized than you'd ever thought possible. Our business is a real business—you're talking about tangible assets. LIV alone does over $40 million a year. That's a real asset. We're dealing with those kinds of big numbers, and it's a serious responsibility on my shoulders.

But having Michael, who is the president of Live Nation, as a partner has been incredible. When I was having some challenges and disputes with someone I've been partners with for a long time, being able to have Live Nation in my corner made me feel stronger. I had them as a partner to help guide me through the whole process.

Any time there's an opening, any time there's a high-stress situation, being able to have Michael coach and counsel me—having a level-headed person who's not emotionally attached to the situation—that's been really good for me. It's like having a mentor who's also your business partner. He's seen every kind of situation, every kind of challenge. He can help me see around corners, avoid pitfalls, think through scenarios I might not have considered.

And the resources that come with being part of Live Nation are incredible. The network, the expertise, the infrastructure—it's like having a whole team of specialists at your disposal. Legal, finance, marketing, operations—whatever you need, they've got world-class people who've done it before.

The flip side is that everything has to be more buttoned up. You can't just handshake deals anymore. You can't just wing it. Everything has to be documented, approved, run through the proper channels. It's more bureaucratic, but it's also more professional. It's the difference between owning a small business and heading up a real company. I love it because in a lot of ways it's the culmination of how I've always done business. The reason why I think I've been so successful is that I'm up early in the morning after a big night. I have a drive every day to show up and give it my all, not just ride coattails. I want to know what worked, what didn't work, what we can do better next time. When we opened

Komodo in Las Vegas at the end of 2023, I was thrilled, but I was also contemplating my future.

When someone asks me what I'd say to someone who's thinking about doing an exit in terms of choosing the right partner, my advice is simple: Take time to really evaluate them. Don't just go for the biggest number.

I've had people along the way say to me, "Can we buy Live Nation out? Can we give you a better deal?" And I'm like, no way. I'm so happy with my partner. It's not even about the money anymore.

The money is important, don't get me wrong. But once you get past a certain threshold, once you know you're going to be financially secure, it becomes about so much more than that. It becomes about trust. It becomes about shared vision. It becomes about having someone in your corner who understands your business, who respects what you've built, and who wants to help you take it to the next level instead of just milking it for short-term profits.

And you know what's great? Michael saw that I had a growing interest in venture capital, and he encouraged me to pursue investing in other companies, supporting me any way he could. The fact that he took the time to see what I was getting excited about and then acted on it means so much to me.

That's the kind of partner you want. Someone who's paying attention to your growth, your interests, your ambitions. Someone who wants to help you become the best version of yourself, not just squeeze the most money out of your existing business.

I see the deals that the people in my world have with their partners, and I know how lucky I am to have chosen the partner I did. Some of them are constantly fighting about strategy. Some of them have partners who are micromanaging every decision. Some of them have partners who don't understand the business and are always second-guessing the expertise that made the company valuable in the first place.

And I think that's something very special about what I have with Michael and his team. They bought my company because they believed in what I was doing. And then they continued to believe in me, continued to support me, continued to give me the resources and freedom to do what I do best.

That's rare. That's not something you find every day. And that's not something you give up just because someone else offers you a few extra million.

What this experience taught me is that loyalty works both ways. I take that same approach with DJs and artists and friends. I've put them in deals not just because I think it's great for them but because it also makes them see me as an entrepreneur and investor who will help lead the next generation. When you give people ownership, when you give them a piece of the upside, they don't just work for you, they work with you.

They protect the brand. They think long-term. They make better decisions because they have skin in the game. And when opportunities come up, they think about what's best for the collective, not just what's best for them personally.

I think that's kind of cool for me, too, because I want to be positioned as not just a nightlife guy. I've worked so hard to not be just a nightlife guy but to be a hospitality guy, and now I just want to be known as more of an entrepreneur in hospitality. Taking the leap into partnering with Live Nation is one of the big things that's going to help me get there because now it's not just me anymore.

The truth is, a successful exit isn't about *leaving* the game. It's about evolving in it. The money is great, but the real win is freedom. The freedom to build differently. To partner smarter. To back the next version of you.

So build it right. Sell it smart. And then? Go again.

That's how you leave what you built without regret.

CHAPTER TEN

BETTING ON PEOPLE

I kind of backed into the world of venture capital. It wasn't something I planned for when I got started thirty years ago, but now it's a huge part of my ecosystem and one I'm excited to see expand in the future.

Right before COVID hit, I started noticing a shift. Brands began coming to me—not the big, established players but the startups, the ones scraping to make a name for themselves. They'd say, "Hey, we see you have a great network. Is there a way you can help us build our brand?" At first, I didn't fully get it. Why would I take equity—a share of their company—instead of just cash up front? It sounded risky, like gambling on something uncertain.

But then I started to spend time with founders. I saw their hustle, the long hours, the passion, the belief in what they were building. That was the part that got me. I realized this wasn't just about selling a product or adding another item to the menu. It was about becoming part of a bigger story, a potential success that I could help shape.

That's really what venture capital is all about. It's an investment approach focused on startups and early-stage companies with high growth potential. Instead of buying a finished product or a proven business, venture capitalists invest money in exchange for equity—ownership stakes—in companies that might be risky but could also grow exponentially. The goal is to back the right founders and ideas early, helping them scale and succeed, and eventually reap the rewards if the company has a successful acquisition or exit.

Venture capital looks like a mix of relationship-building, mentorship, and risk-taking. Unlike a traditional loan, which must be paid back regardless of how the business does, VC money is a bet on the future. Investors become partners, often working closely with founders to provide guidance, open doors to networks, and offer strategic advice. It's not just about the cash; it's about adding value beyond the check.

In my case, it's been about spotting brands that align with my hospitality experience and intuition. When I say yes to investing, I'm not just betting on a product but on the people behind it—their vision, grit, and adaptability. The energy that founders bring is contagious, and being part of their journey is exciting. Sometimes the companies are in food and beverage, sometimes in tech, but the throughline is innovation and drive.

Venture capital isn't for everyone, though. It requires a tolerance for risk because many startups fail or take years to become profitable. But for those that do succeed, the returns can be substantial, not just financially but in terms of impact and legacy. It's about helping build something from the ground up, watching a seed idea grow into a thriving company.

Looking back, I never planned on becoming a venture capitalist or angel investor, but now I see it as a way to leverage my experience and network to help the next generation of entrepreneurs. It's a dynamic, challenging, and rewarding part of my career that continues to teach me a lot about business, people, and the future of industries I care about.

I've always loved brand building. I'm a hospitality guy, sure, but I also understand lifestyle, because lifestyle is such a huge part of hospitality. I've spent decades getting to know my guests, anticipating what they'll like and what they want more of, so it makes sense. Who better to introduce new ideas to them than me? When a brand fits into the world I've built, I know I can help make it explode. So I started thinking: What if instead of just putting their stuff in my places, I also built actual partnerships with people I was excited about? Part of what allowed me to do this was my partnership with Michael Rapino, because having him involved with Groot Hospitality has given me so many great resources; and through hospitality, I'm able to connect those resources with some of the great people I meet on a regular basis. I'm looking at about ten deals a week now. Founders pitching me on everything from new venue concepts to tech platforms to consumer products. DJs asking me to invest in their tequila brands. Real estate guys calling me to co-develop new hotels. It's a completely different world than the one I was in when I was just owning venues.

But I'm selective. I'm not just writing checks because I can. I'm looking for opportunities where I can add real value, where my experience and network can actually help the business succeed. Instead of just building my own businesses, I'm helping other people build theirs. And what's great is that I get to be the person I wish I had when I was starting out. I get to be the guy who understands the business, who's been through the ups and downs, who can help navigate the challenges that come with building something from scratch.

My first big investment was with a brand called Gopuff, a delivery app that's like having your go-to convenience store inside your phone. I met Raf and Yakir, the founders, a few years back, and from the minute I sat down with them, I knew they were different. Not different like "cool startup guys" or "tech bros in vests" different. I mean like scrappy, smart, humble—like they'd already survived five lifetimes of business drama and were still somehow not jaded.

The product itself is amazing. It's fast, they have an amazing selection of products, and I can get all my weird snacks and late-night cravings delivered without moving from the couch. But that's not why I invested. I invested because of Raf and Yakir. When we first met, they started telling me how they launched Gopuff out of their college dorm room. The way they tell it, they hated going to

7-Eleven, but late at night, when you're studying or coming home from a party, what other options are there? They weren't impressed with the delivery landscape, either. So they came up with this idea to build a totally vertically integrated model—own the fulfillment centers, own the inventory, own the delivery. This was 2013, by the way. They were nineteen. Every venture capitalist in the world was like, "What are you doing? Why would you buy stuff? Why would you own things?" It was a model a lot of people in the tech and commerce worlds weren't interested in.

But Raf and Yakir just didn't care. They knew what they needed to do to make it work for the user—and that meant owning everything.

So what did they do? They bootstrapped it. No outside money. Not at first. You want to hear hustle? These guys were literally selling used office furniture from companies going out of business. And they did the first deliveries themselves. Driving around in a Plymouth Voyager, just trying to make it work. One of their first deliveries, they got T-boned by another car, and what does Raf do? He doesn't call 911. He grabs the bag from the backseat and runs a mile to the customer's house. Scratched up, dazed, whatever—it didn't matter. The customer? Still ordering from them eleven years later.

You hear that and you know these guys are not normal. They're in it to build something real, and those are the kinds of people I've always been drawn to.

What really impressed me was how they scaled. They didn't do it like everyone else. They built micro-fulfillment centers—what they call MFCs—all over. That's where all the stuff comes from. They stock the warehouses themselves, and because of that, it's faster, cheaper, and more efficient. They make money on the products, not just the delivery fees.

They always say it: "We monetize products, not people."

And look, they had no money for a long time. There was a point where they literally lived in their fulfillment centers. Raf in Boston. Yakir in Philly. They couldn't afford rent. They were running customer service themselves. Phones would go from Raf to Yakir to his cousin Simon. Everybody was doing everything—packing, driving, talking to customers. Full-on all-in.

Their first investor found them because the interns at his firm were ordering Gopuff and figured out they hadn't raised any money. He calls the customer service line, and Raf picks up the phone. The guy's like, "Wait, you're the founder? Why are you answering the phone?" And Raf just goes, "We do everything here."

Even after raising $50 or $60 million, they hit a point where they were a month away from running out of cash. And they had a deal on the table—serious money—but the investor wanted control of the company. They could've taken it. It would've saved them. But Yakir looks at Raf and goes, "If I don't get to run this business with you, I don't want to run it at all."

And Raf's like, "You're crazy." But he tells the investor, "No deal—not if it would require us to give up this much."

An hour later? The investor calls back. "Okay, we'll do it on your terms."

That's what I'm talking about.

Control matters. Protecting the founders matters. And that's why when I get a brand pitch, I always say the same thing: "Do you mind if I get the Gopuff founders on the phone?"

And you should see their faces. These kids are, like, vibrating. Because nobody gets to talk to Raf and Yakir directly. It's like ten layers of gatekeepers just to get a meeting. But I make the call, we loop them in, and guess what? Instead of crushing these little brands, we help them. Raf looks at their contracts, their structures, gives them real feedback. He'll tell a founder, "Hey, you need to add this clause to protect yourself. You don't want to be the guy who starts a company and ends up with nothing." They've amassed so much data about users, and for a brand founder to be able to talk to them directly, to have one-on-one conversations with a platform that serves as a major distribution point, is life-changing.

The most important thing about investing, to me, is continuing to expand my ecosystem, and it's all about finding people I want to invest in—the products have to be good, too, but if I don't connect with the people, I know it's not going to be a good fit.

I've bet on people whose products I wasn't even sure about, but I knew they had it in them. Like Liquid Death. A water company called Liquid Death? Water in tallboy cans with a crazy logo? Come on. During the pandemic, we're like, "No way this works." But the founder, Mike, just had the it factor—there was something about this guy that made me want to be in business with him, so we did it. Now you can't go to a party or a concert or a festival or a club without seeing a hundred people drinking those cans of water.

I say this all the time: "The best brands make other brands better." That's how you grow. That's how you create an ecosystem. Not by extracting value but by building it—together.

Sometimes when I'm making a connection, someone will ask, "What's in it for you?" And I'm like, "Nothing. I just want to see it win. I want to see you win." That's it—though I do get free Gopuff for life.

The key for me when I'm considering working with a brand is this: It has to make sense in my ecosystem. I don't just invest in things because they might blow up. I want to know I can help them blow up. I want to be able to put something in my venues, wear it, taste it, use it, show it to my audience. That's what makes me valuable to these companies. I'm not a silent investor. I'm not the guy who wires money and disappears. I'm involved. Over the years I've made a lot of friends, and a lot of those friends have millions of followers on social media. If I'm investing in a company, I want the product to be something my friends are genuinely excited to use and post about.

A few years ago, my team and I sat down and came up with a plan: "Let's pick a brand. Let's push it together. Let's own it together." I was looking for a lifestyle brand, but it was important to me to pick something that felt authentically me, and I landed on

Prince, the tennis brand. It had that Americana vibe—you'd see it at country clubs, and it reminded me of the '80s and '90s when Andre Agassi was the biggest tennis player in the world and also a total rock star. When the opportunity came up to become part of Prince, I thought, "Why not?" I might not have been a tennis fanatic, but I remembered the brand and its potential. We could make it cool again.

So I partnered with Prince. At first, I focused more on the off-court lifestyle side of things. I wasn't trying to compete with Nike or Wilson on their turf. That's not the game I play. I play the cultural relevance game. I'd send gear out to celebrities and influencers. We didn't sign contracts with dedicated brand ambassadors because, honestly, we couldn't afford them like the other brands anyway. But I'd send hundreds of boxes, handwritten notes included, and then just wait to see if they posted about it on social media. I knew there was a good chance they'd be rocking Prince merch courtesy of yours truly.

Through this, I developed a relationship with the Bollettieri family—the best tennis coaches in history. That sparked my own interest in playing tennis. Now, I play tennis regularly with some of the top twenty players in the world, and I always make sure Prince gear is on the court with them. It's wild to me—I'll hop on Instagram and see Grand Slam winners sharing clips of themselves hitting unreal shots in Prince outfits while I post about being a dedicated player but a regular guy, trying to hit against someone who's literally won at Wimbledon. Tennis has become an obsession. I play every day now, and I care as much about what happens on the court as off it. The first time I really played, at Amanyara in Turks and Caicos, it was love at first serve. I was just hitting the ball with a trainer, and suddenly I felt that topspin. I'm hooked now. And once you get passionate about something like that, it doesn't feel like something you have to balance anymore. It just feels right—like an obvious part of your life. Now, every day, I'm so excited to play. I remember going to the French Open to support my friend Stan Wawrinka, a Swiss tennis player. I thought I'd be there for an hour, but it turned into five full hours. The heat was intense; you couldn't move. But then, fast forward to last summer when I was a total tennis freak. I went to Wimbledon and other tournaments, and it was totally different. I wanted more than just five hours of tennis. The whole experience had changed because I was invested.

Prince itself is doing incredibly well. We've done collections with brands like Brooks Brothers, Sporty & Rich, Happy Dad, and other big fashion brands. It's the same philosophy I honed at Velvet Lounge all those years ago—building collaborations with other brands helps build our brand equity. That's what I mean when I say I incorporate everything into my lifestyle. If I'm into it, I'll sell it better than anybody else. This isn't just about tennis gear; it's about the whole culture around it.

Reebok made these special sneakers for me as part of a promotional campaign, and I started talking with them. I was like, "Why don't we do a Prince Reebok?" Back in the day, tennis player Michael Chang, a big Prince guy, also worked with Reebok, and it felt like an organic connection. It turned out to be a really cool collaboration for me. I thought it was next level—another iconic brand excited to work with Prince. That felt really rewarding.

Tennis itself is such a social sport. It really puts you in the perfect position to make connections. I've built so many great relationships on the tennis court. People come and train with me for an hour, we play some tennis, and our connections become stronger and more organic. It's incredible how much business flow I get from the court. Tennis has become a real platform for me, not just for the love of the game but for connecting with people in a fun space.

I'm most excited about keeping that momentum going. We're not just selling rackets and track suits; we're selling a true lifestyle brand. I've gone from someone who barely followed the sport to someone who lives it, breathes it, and uses it as a platform for cultural relevance and business. Prince has become a major part of my lifestyle and my business, and I'm excited to see where we can take it next.

I meet with so many founders, and a lot of them think they're sitting on gold. They'll say their company is worth a billion dollars, and I'll just smile and say, "Okay." But valuation isn't just what you say it is. It's what someone's willing to pay. It's whether the brand has a runway. Is there real momentum here, or are you just early and loud?

I've had some zeros and I've had some unicorns. And I've

learned to ask the same few questions every time. What can I add to this? Do I bring value? Can I share insights that will really take this brand over the top? Most importantly, are these people I like and actively want to be in business with?

Take Vacation, for example. They do sunscreen products with a retro-style branding that looks straight out of the 1980s—also known as one of my favorite eras of all time (seriously, if you follow me on social media, you know I love to post clips of random *Miami Vice* episodes). I took an advisory deal with them alongside my investment, which basically means you're officially brought on to provide guidance and expertise to a company—helping them with strategy, connections, and advice—while staying focused on high-level decision-making as opposed to day-to-day operations. It's usually a set period where you commit some time and knowledge, often in exchange for shares or compensation.

Honestly, I liked working with them so much that I completely forgot the advisory deal even ended. I was just genuinely invested in their success and stayed involved naturally. Then, when the term was up, they came back to me and said, "Hey, we want to give you more advisory shares. You've done so much for us. We want to keep you on." That was a great feeling—knowing my input mattered and they wanted me to continue to be part of their journey.

I mean, that's the highest compliment. When a founder wants you in, not because they have to but because they know how much you've moved the needle, that's the kind of energy I love.

I'm big on looking people directly in the eye—if I'm going to bet on something, I want to see the crazy in them. Because let's be real: Founders are crazy. They're dropping out of Yale to work full-time on their ideas. Who walks away from a Yale degree to launch a sparkling soda company? If my daughters ever did that, I'd go nuts! But as an investor, I'm into that kind of crazy.

I recently got offered the chance to be involved in two deals around the same time—a beverage company I won't name, and OLIPOP, a healthy soda with flavors like root beer, grape, and orange cream—nostalgic flavors that reminded me of being a kid. The other brand was at a $25 million valuation. OLIPOP was at $125 million. Most people would say, "That's a no-brainer. Take the lower valuation." But even though OLIPOP was four, five times more expensive on paper, I loved the product. The flavors were just better. I thought, "If I'm going to have a fridge full of this stuff and give it to people, I want to be proud of it. I want to drink it." And even though the other company had a huge exit recently, I still don't think I made the wrong call. I didn't love the flavors, and so partnering with them wouldn't be authentic to me. I think OLIPOP is going to have an even bigger exit. That's the thing about investing—you're betting on taste, and you're betting on grit and on someone's ability to be fearless.

I'm also looking for companies and brands that can naturally slide into partnerships with my existing portfolio. I'm obsessed with strong flavors. I always have been. And Fly By Jing—founded by the amazing chef and cookbook author Jing Gao—is just. . . next level. Her company went from a Kickstarter campaign to national distribution to being in every cool person's pantry. I helped bring it into the hospitality world, and from there, it just caught on. I asked for a sample to be sent to me before our first call, and when I tasted it, I knew it was something I wanted to get behind.

In the beginning, I was doing small checks. Little advisory pieces. But now? I'm trying to do fewer deals but go bigger. Bigger checks, bigger pieces, more influence. I want to work with brands where I can move the culture. The other cool part? I get to meet some of the best entrepreneurs in the world. People who leave it all behind to try to build something new. That takes guts. Whether it's sunscreen, soda, chili crisp, or tennis gear—what I'm really investing in is belief. In themselves. In their product. And in the idea that they can make something where there was nothing before.

The hardest thing for me, honestly, has been learning how to say no. In hospitality, if someone brings you an idea and you see even the tiniest spark, you're conditioned to say, "Let's try it." Let's build the pop-up. Let's do the party. Let's create the dish. But in investing? That approach can burn you. Time is limited. Capital is limited. If you say yes too much, you end up diluted—your attention, your energy, your network.

I had to train myself to recognize when I liked the vibe but not the opportunity.

There was a brand I almost invested in. Beautiful branding. Founder had the look. Everyone was talking about it. But when I dug in? They didn't have a supply chain figured out. Their margins were brutal. They were basically paying people to take product. And I had to ask myself: Do I want to spend the next three years teaching someone how to run a business? Or do I want to back someone who already knows?

I passed. Still wish them well. But I don't invest to babysit. I invest to amplify.

I'm also very careful about doing deals with my friends, because those opportunities come up a lot. My relationships are everything to me, and I'd never want to fall out with anyone over a deal or make a connection I didn't think was a natural fit—remember how upset I was about that boat? It's always important to me to be transparent, and I'm really careful about that when I'm involved with any kind of deal. Something that comes up a lot when you get into investing is the SPV—special purpose vehicle. SPVs are legal entities created to pool money for one investment. And sometimes people try to use them to make money off their friends. Like, "Hey, I'll let you in on this deal . . . for a fee." Let me be clear about something: I don't put friends into SPVs. Ever. To me, that's offensive. If I find a great investment, I share it with my friends. I say, "This is amazing. You should get in." I don't take a cut. I don't mark it up. That's gross.

Someone tried to SPV me once. Someone I considered a friend. And I was like, are you kidding me? That kind of behavior is a dealbreaker. I'm not doing this to nickel-and-dime people. Yeah, making money is important, but how you conduct yourself is the most important thing. I'm doing this because I love building things, and you can't build anything without basic trust and respect.

Now I run every opportunity through a filter. I ask myself the following:

Do I actually love the product?

Can I authentically integrate this into my world?

Do I want to have dinner with the founder?

Do they have the infrastructure to scale?

Is there a meaningful brand story?

If I can't say yes to at least four out of five, I walk. That's how I've stayed aligned. Because the truth is, everything I invest in reflects on me. If I'm telling people, "This is the next big thing," and it turns out to be garbage? That's not just on the founder; that's on me. I also want founders to know who I am. Whenever I'm in serious talks with a company, I'll send founders a list of the forty companies I've invested in and their founder's names and cell phone numbers. I say, "Call whomever you want from all the brands I've invested in and ask them about my commitment." I have enough confidence in what I do that I don't want to be in a relationship without trust. When you approach deals in that way, it changes the negotiations, because they see that you're so self-assured that you're willing to bet on yourself. From there, we can build a solid foundation. We grow each other's ecosystems and, from there, I really believe there's nothing we can't do.

People always ask me, "How do you find these deals?"

The answer is: I don't chase. I curate.

Some of them come through relationships—friends of friends, founders I've helped in the past who make intros. But a lot of it just shows up. People pitch me all the time. DMs, emails, people cornering me at events. And I can usually tell in the first sixty seconds if there's something there.

I look at their deck. I try the product. I call them up and just talk. No suits, no jargon. I want to know what they're obsessed with. Because if you're not obsessed, why should I be? If it checks out, we go deeper. Sometimes I'll say, "Let's start small—send me some product. Let me test it in one of my venues." That's what I did with Fly By Jing. And once I saw the reaction, I doubled down. But sometimes I go all in immediately. That's what happened with OLIPOP. I just knew.

I also don't mind writing the "unsexy" checks. Not every deal needs to be a big splash. Some of the best wins are the ones you quietly nurture over time. And yeah, sometimes it flops.

I've had brands that went nowhere. Good product, decent team, but no real traction. Or they scale too fast and implode. Or they take on too much money too early and then get stuck trying to justify inflated valuations.

I've learned that it happens, and you can't let it derail you. Not every idea wins. That's the game.

But what I do take personally is how founders handle failure. The best ones don't hide. They communicate. They own it. They say, "This didn't work—here's what we're trying instead." That kind of transparency? That earns my respect. I'd rather back a founder

185

who failed gracefully than one who "succeeded" by faking their numbers.

Another thing I've realized: Capital is expensive, but community is rare. Founders come to me for money, sure. But more often, they come to me because they want to be part of the world I've built. They want access to my venues, my network, my distribution.

And I love that, because I want to build a community of brands that support each other. Where if I bring in a brand like Vacation, I can pair it with a fragrance collab. Where OLIPOP's launch party happens at my club. Where brands are launching exclusive flavors on GoPuff.

That's the future. It's not just brand building; it's ecosystem building. You get the right group of founders, investors, chefs, creators, and operators in one room? You can make culture shift. That's where the real value is.

I'm not a flipper. I don't invest thinking, "How fast can I triple this?" That mindset kills brands.

I want to build enduring value. Stuff that lasts. Stuff that becomes part of people's lives. When I talk to founders, I ask them: "Are you trying to build a brand, or just trying to build a valuation?" Because that's a different thing. One is substance. The other is smoke.

I want to be part of a generation of brands that make people feel something, and in that sense, I do have a real advantage, which is that I've spent most of my career in the hospitality business, observing people. I see what people eat, drink, wear, talk about.

Every night. Every day. I see what gets Instagrammed. What gets ignored. What gets reordered. What gets dumped.

That kind of data? That's gold.

I know if a product has pull before the data comes in. I see it in the way people react. And that gives me an edge. I can take a new brand and plug it into my venues and immediately know if we've got something. That's why I always say that I don't need a spreadsheet—I need a weekend. If people are coming up to me at the bar asking, "What's that?"—that's traction.

I am the filter. If it doesn't feel authentic to me, I pass because I know myself. If I'm into it, I'll talk about it. I'll text people about it. I'll post about it. I'll pitch it without being asked. But if I'm not into it? I'll ignore it. It'll sit in a corner collecting dust. And then I've wasted your time and mine. So I only invest in things I want to get behind. That's why you see me going so hard for my brands. I believe in them. I use them. I live them. In a lot of ways, working with brands is very similar to what I've been doing for decades with my clubs—sniffing out talent and then figuring out ways for us to mutually grow.

When I think about the DJs I have close relationships with—people like John Summit and Peggy Gou—it's very similar to the relationships I have with brands I invest in. Whenever I was booking an artist to play at LIV—or even further back, to places like Tantra—I was looking for people I really liked. People I'd want to hear play if I was going out.

A huge part of my job has always been keeping my finger on

the pulse of what's exciting, and the way I do that isn't to chase trends. I look at data, of course, and I stay aware of trends; but at the end of the day, I want to build an ecosystem that I'm excited to live in. I want to own restaurants where I love the food and throw events I can really have fun at. When I invest in a brand, I'm investing money, but I'm also investing things that are harder to put a price on: my time, enthusiasm, and ideas.

CHAPTER ELEVEN

THE BALANCING ACT

I love to work. Obviously. I wrote a book about it! I'll never stop working—it's just part of who I am. But being a present husband and father? That's the most important thing to me, hands down. Finding time for everything isn't always easy, though. I've really had to learn how to prioritize.

I met my wife, Isabela, and pretty quickly knew she was The One. She's originally from Brazil, and when we met, she was living in New York. The night we met, she had just gotten back from a photo shoot in LA, and she didn't even feel like going out, but her friends (and fate) convinced her otherwise. I was in New York for work, and I was supposed to go back to Miami the next morning. But when I met Isabela, I knew I had to spend more time with her. I missed my flight (Was it on purpose? I'll never tell.) and promptly asked her to lunch, and we've been inseparable ever since. In 2015, I proposed in Wynwood: I had an artist do a mural that said "Will you marry me? Check yes or no" on one of the walls, and before

I slipped the ring on her finger, I handed her a can of spray paint. We laughed through our happy tears as she sprayed a big "x" in the "yes" box, and the next year we got married in the same spot, an open-air wedding celebration in the middle of Wynwood.

I'm incredibly lucky—I've got a very smart wife who's a real partner in my life and in the business. She's got the best eye. She gives amazing feedback on the food at my restaurants—like, brutally honest when she needs to be—and she picks out all the chinaware and glassware, too. I trust her implicitly, which means I don't really draw a line between personal life and professional life. We're living it all together. I still want to spend as much time with her as possible. I see people in marriages who hate being with each other. They look forward to time away from their spouse. I'm the opposite. I can't wait to be with my wife. I want to do everything with her. We have a rule that we never spend more than five days away from each other, which means we travel as a family a lot. It makes trips for work even more fun, honestly. She'll come with me to Las Vegas and bring the girls and her friends and turn it into a whole experience. She's a real girl's girl and she's a great hostess, and I think when people meet her, they like me even more.

Isabela is also an entrepreneur herself. She just launched her own clothing and jewelry brands, and they're doing incredibly well. She's also the face of and an advisor and investor in IGK Hair, and she didn't take any help from me. Didn't ask, didn't need to. In fact, now I'm her plus-one sometimes, which is awesome. I'm so proud of her whenever a brand comes to her and asks her to work with them, because her first reaction is always, "I'm not interested in the fee. I'm interested in the equity." She's a powerhouse in her own right, not "David Grutman's wife."

She also loves to invest her own money. Like, if I invest a million dollars in a brand, she'll put in a hundred grand of her own, and I'll be like, "Babe, I just invested in this for us," and she'll say, "Yeah, well that's our money. What's yours is ours and what's mine is mine." I love that. She's not just interested in the stock market—she's putting her time and money into brands and other entrepreneurs. This is one of my most important pieces of advice: If you want work–life balance, marry someone who is going to be your partner in every aspect of life. Someone who makes you better at what you do. Someone who inspires you. Not just someone who tolerates your schedule or your ambition. Isabela gets it. She understands the late nights and the constant motion and the vision. She sees the big picture. And now that she's got her own thing going, I understand her even better, too. We trade advice. We push each other. We celebrate wins and we talk through problems. It's a real partnership.

My team trusts and respects her, too. They go to her for opinions, and she's usually right. I see how much value she brings not just to our home life but to my companies, too. And I don't take that for granted. It's a gift, and it's helped me understand that balance isn't always about stepping away from work (I do think that's important, too, though it's hard for me to take my own advice here). It's about integrating it into a life you love.

* * *

I love talking business with Isabela, but I love raising our daughters, Kaia and Vida, together even more. It's funny—when Isabela was pregnant with Kaia, I was so nervous about being a first-time dad to a little girl, but it came so naturally to me once she was born. When we started talking about having a second a few years later, I knew I wanted another girl—being a girl dad was my destiny, and I got my wish when Vida was born. Being their dad has changed the way I deal with people. A few years after they were born, a female lawyer on my team made a mistake and I got really angry—like, I was ready to blow up even though I'm not a big yeller. But then she said something to me that stuck: "Would you let anyone talk to your girls that way?" And from that moment on, I realized I could never raise my voice at her or anyone else. I can never do anything like that anymore. I wouldn't want anyone talking to my daughter the way I was upset and about to talk to this person, and now I enter every conversation with that mindset: Would I want someone to talk to my daughters the way I'm about to talk to this person? It's changed everything about how I handle people.

I swear, these girls have already seen more of the world than I had by the time I was twenty-five. Saudi Arabia, Egypt, Italy, Japan—you name it, they've been there. We bring them on probably 90 percent of our trips. People ask how we balance it all, and I always say that we do it together.

The coolest part, though, is that my girls get to see their mom build businesses. That's the example they're getting every day.

That work and life and family don't have to be in conflict. That your partner can be your biggest inspiration.

I drive the girls to school every morning. That time with them, just us in the car, is some of the most valuable time of my whole day. I know that sounds like a cliché, and trust me, it's hard for me to give them my full attention sometimes. I've always got a million things going through my head. Texts, emails, deals, ideas. It's nonstop. But I've learned to carve out specific moments. Like at night, before they go to sleep, we all crawl into the bed and watch a little TV together. Lately, as they're getting older, we've been having these great little conversations about life and the world. They surprise me with how much they pick up on.

We also make sure they're part of our world. We're involved in nonprofits and giving back, and I love that they get to experience that for themselves. I want them to understand gratitude. I want them to see giving back in action. I will not raise entitled kids. It's tempting sometimes, I'm not gonna lie. We go into a toy store and I want to buy them everything. I worked so hard to get to a place where I can. But Isabela? She's strict. She's like, "Nope, one toy." And she's right. She's 100 percent right. She's on the board of Style Saves, a nonprofit in Miami that helps kids get access to school supplies and other necessities, and recently she helped run a huge event that took over the Miami Convention Center for a full weekend and set up 25,000 kids with everything they needed to start the school year. Many of the brands I work with contributed, and we had our daughters there both days. It was so special to watch them learn the importance of giving back and to realize that they have a real responsibility to do good in the world.

I'm so proud that my daughters get to see a relationship that's rooted in mutual respect. I want them to grow up knowing that their mom is a boss. She's not waiting around for permission. She's taking risks, launching products, building a following, and making moves. And she's doing it all while being an incredible mother, wife, and partner. That's the model I want them to have. Not some fantasy about having to choose between ambition and family—but the truth, which is you can have both if you build your life with intention.

And listen, it's not perfect. There are hard days. There are nights where I'm on my phone too much or days when I miss bedtime because of a dinner. But overall? I'm present. I'm trying. And that's what matters.

I used to have this boat at my old house. My favorite thing to do when people came to visit Miami was take them out on the boat, give them the full Miami Beach tour. It wasn't just showing off—it was a way to connect. Today, although Groot Hospitality has an office, I mostly work from home, and it's become a thing that everyone I'm meeting with has to come by the house. We'll have green juice, I'll insist you try one of the hundred beverages in my fridge, and we'll sit at my dining room table while we talk. My Australian shepherd, Kona, will probably be sitting at your feet.

Another thing I love about working from home is that it gives me more time with my daughters. They'll come home from school and tell me about what they learned or from jiu-jitsu practice and show me their newest moves. They also love to introduce themselves to whomever is over, which I love—they know how to shake hands and nicely share their names. It doesn't matter what I'm doing—I could be in the middle of a meeting trying to close a billion-dollar deal. If my girls want to come give me a hug and a kiss, that's what I'm doing.

There's this misconception people have—especially in hospitality— that if you're successful, you must be constantly on, always working, and totally unavailable to your family. Like, there's no way you can be owning restaurants, nightclubs, events, deals, and also have time to take your kids to school or help your wife with her brand. And yeah, I get that. It's intense. The pace is crazy. But what people don't always see is how intentional I am with my time. I incorporate my family into my business, which allows me to live a life where I'm always giving 100 percent to both.

I think about it constantly. Am I really showing up in this moment? Am I giving my kids a version of me that isn't distracted and thinking about the next opening? Am I being a supportive husband, not just in a financial or business sense but emotionally? Because you can be around someone all day and still not *be* with them. I don't want that. I'm lucky that I've created systems that allow for this kind of life. I've got a great team.

And let me say this: Being a dad has made me better at business. I'm more empathetic. I listen better. I've learned how to explain things clearly and calmly, because when you've had to explain to a six-year-old why she can't have cookies for breakfast, explaining a staffing challenge to your marketing team feels easy. Patience is a muscle, and my kids help me flex it every single day.

Plus, there's something about seeing the world through their eyes. When we travel, it's not just about hitting all the restaurants or networking or checking in on projects. It's about seeing pyramids for the first time, or trying new snacks in Japan, or watching them dance around a hotel room in Rome. Those moments make the hustle worth it. And they remind me what I'm working for—not just the wins but the memories.

We talk a lot in hospitality about "guest experience"—how we make people feel. But we don't talk enough about our experience. What does it feel like to be us? To be public-facing, constantly networking, solving problems, building brands—but also building families? Because it's a lot. And the pressure's real.

There was a time when I used to think that in order to be successful, I had to be everywhere, say yes to everything. But I also don't want to live my life with regret, and when you find yourself spread too thin, those regrets stack up. So now I say no a lot more, not to be rude but to protect what matters most.

Every morning at eight o'clock, no matter what, I'm on the tennis court. Even if I've been working until three or four in the morning, I still show up at eight to play tennis. Then, every evening at six, I do my weights. I keep those as my boundaries. Knowing I have tennis at eight in the morning means there are certain things I just won't do late at night.

Work–life balance is a moving target. Some weeks I nail it. Some weeks I'm a mess. But I keep showing up. I keep adjusting. And I keep remembering what matters: my family, my beliefs, and building a life that makes room for both the grind and the good stuff.

I want to be the kind of dad who feels fun to his kids. Who's not just there to say no, or teach them lessons, or drive them around. I want to be someone they remember laughing with. Someone they're excited to be around.

And the same goes for my marriage. We've got all these over-lapping areas—parenting, business, social stuff—but we also carve out time for just us. No kids, no work talk, no phones. Just a dinner, or a walk, or a trip where we get to be partners, best friends, people in love. That part matters. You can't let that get buried under all the logistics.

Now don't get me wrong. There are chaotic weeks. Times when I'm pulled in ten different directions. Times when my schedule has me in meetings from seven o'clock in the morning until the sun goes down. I'm not some perfectly balanced zen guy all the time, but I try to be mindful.

And listen, I get that not everyone has the same resources I do. It's easier to talk about balance when you've got help, when you can afford childcare or travel or nights out. But no matter where you are in life or what stage you're at, I think the core idea still applies: Time is your most precious currency. How you spend it is everything. Even if it's just ten minutes of quality time. Even if it's one night a week where you really unplug. Even if it's texting your partner in the middle of a crazy day to say, "Thinking of you." Those things add up. That's balance.

And if you're building something—whether it's a brand, a business, or a life—don't forget who you're building it for. Don't lose the plot.

I used to think that legacy was all about empire. Big projects. Big names. Big wins. But now, I think legacy is everything I'm building to live way longer than I will. It's how your team describes you after a tough day, and it's knowing that you've done your best in all your relationships. That when your name comes up, people only have good things to say. That's what sticks.

So yeah, I love to work. I'll never stop working. And as crazy as my life can get, I wouldn't trade it for anything, because the moments I've had with my wife and daughters? Every time I'm sitting on the floor watching a movie with my girls or walking into an event while the photographers yell at me to move out of the way so they can get the perfect shot of Isabela? That's the real reward. That's the win.

CONCLUSION

THE BEST IS YET TO COME

Ah, the last chapter of the book. The moment when I wrap everything up in a neat little bow and send you on your way to take the lessons I have learned and apply them to your own life. It's a special moment! It also means I have to answer a question I get asked a lot: What's next for me?

The truth is, I'm still figuring it out, but I've got a few ideas.

First, let me say this: I'm not slowing down anytime soon. I know I'll be signing twenty-year leases when I'm seventy. That's just who I am. This isn't about retiring or even easing off the gas. It's about evolving. I'm always evolving. That's what keeps me going.

Right now, one of the things I'm most proud of is "The David Grutman Experience," the course I've spent several years teaching at Florida International University (FIU). It focuses on entrepreneurship and what it really takes to conceptualize and create a leading hospitality platform. Not just what they put in textbooks but the stuff I've learned from actually doing it. The relationship building, the instincts, the "How do I get this deal done when it seems impossible" kind of thing. The truth is, when they first approached me about doing the class, I said no. I had too much on my plate already, and besides, what did I know about teaching? They kept on me, though, and after five years of teaching the class they even gave me a doctorate, so now I can technically call myself Doctor David Grutman. Not bad for a kid who got kicked out of his high school for launching fireworks into the toilet, right?

Last year, we had 450 students enrolled. Every week we tackle a different topic in the world of hospitality, and I bring in a special guest or two, people at the top of their games, across industries. I want my students to learn from the best. It's so fun to see them excited to ask questions, and they're good ones, too. They're not just there to get a look at someone famous—they want to learn everything they can. I call this generation the "hustle generation," and it's so cool to be someone they look up to. I love knowing that in ten years, these kids are going to be out making their own marks.

I gave the commencement speech at FIU in April 2024, which I'm incredibly proud of because I think it speaks to both my legacy and to the fact that I'm still learning and growing, too. That's part of what feels so special about playing the long game for me—it's being excited that there's always another place for me to go.

Over the next five to ten years, I want to create legacy venues—restaurants and clubs that continue to be important parts of the hospitality landscape for decades to come. I'm thinking about scaling brands like Komodo, Gekkō, and Papi Steak into multiple locations. I've already got the playbook; now it's about putting the right people in the right places and growing with integrity. Because it's not just about making money; it's about creating experiences people remember forever.

I love Miami, and I love Las Vegas, and I love Dallas, but I also want to be worldwide. I've spent time in Saudi Arabia and the UAE, and I'm very inspired every time I go. There are some very cool opportunities over there, and I'm branching out—restaurants, resorts, experiences. I want to be part of that wave.

People come to me to have fun—to go out, to celebrate, to escape. It's an entertainment experience. It's over the top. That's always been my lane. Nineteen years in, LIV is still one of the hottest nightclubs out there. But I've always had this itch, this desire to elevate even further. To not just be thought of as high-end or trendy but as truly luxurious and aspirational.

There's a difference between "this is cool" and "this is iconic." And I want iconic. I want that powerhouse lunch, that impossible-to-get dinner reservation, that brand that becomes shorthand for luxury. That's the bar I'm aiming for.

Right now, the focus is on building a luxury members-only club. A place with exclusive energy, not just about the space but about the community. And from there, I want to turn that membership into something even bigger—residences. Something like that would be a true stamp. That's longevity. That's a lifestyle brand people want to live inside.

And I think I can get there by cultivating a lifestyle that incorporates so much of what I'm already doing. People who are buying into this way of living—the energy, the vibe, the values. I don't think anyone's created the definitive hospitality-residence-luxury-lifestyle hybrid for this generation. And I want to be the one to do it. I've got five years in my head as the working window to make this happen.

In ten years? We'll see. I'll be sixty then, and I don't know what rate I'll be moving at, though I hope it's still a fast one.

I also hope I'm continuing to watch the companies I invest in grow and that I'm continuing to learn from them. This new generation doesn't want to work nine to five. Those days are done. They're not waiting forty years for a gold watch. They've got platforms, they've got tools, they've got access. They want to build something of their own. And I respect that.

In fact, I think this entrepreneurial spirit is contagious. You see someone else doing it, and suddenly you realize you can do it, too. That's what I want to foster. That's what I want to amplify.

I don't know the exact blueprint, but I know the direction.

Legacy. Luxury. Lifestyle. Longevity.

I want to keep building brands that matter. Telling stories that stick, creating spaces that feel like magic, and doing it all with the people I love by my side.

I'm playing the long game—and I think you can, too.

ACKNOWLEDGMENTS

Thank you to everyone who made this book possible: my family, Isabela, Kaia, and Vida Grutman, Kim Kardashian, Angela Serratore, Sabrina Taitz, Chad Fabrikant, Sarah Ried, Sarah Goldstein, Jennifer Freilach, Nathalie Ramirez, Zoey Cole, Sam Mitchell, Ashley Alberico, Andrew Rein, Molly Stern, Ari Emanuel, Ben Simone and Adam Harris & the WME team, the Groot Hospitality team, Max Pallot, my LIV family, the Komodo family, Alex Pirez & Nick Smith, Mike & Chloe Kimel, Kendall Jenner, Khloé Kardashian , Kris Jenner, Dakota Green, Lach Hall, John Shahidi, Sam Shahidi, Kyle Forgeard, Dean Michael Cheng & Shivani Joshi at Florida International University, Michael Rapino, Jordan Zachary, Hamed Fayez, Prince Bader Al Saud, Bruno Soares, Osgemeos, John Hopmans, Matthew Hansen, Mitchell Littman, Neil Fagen and the legal team, Jonathan "Foodgod" Cheban, Jony Ive, Christopher Wilson, and the LoveFrom team, Shep Gordon, JR, Jeff Soffer, Brett Mufson, Phil Goldfarb and the Fontainebleau team, David Einhorn, Noah & Melissa Tepperberg, Jason Strauss, Burt Rapoport, Pharrell Williams, Rafael Ilishayev, Yakir Gola & Gopuff, Matthew Salter, Corey Salter, Jamie Salter, David Beckham and Victoria Beckham, David

ACKNOWLEDGMENTS

Gardner, Alix Earle, Gary & Madison Brecka, Shawn Sullivan at Rockwell Group, Michael Gardner, Ken Fulk, Rebeca León, Anitta, David Guetta, Michael Bay, Seth Browarnik, Raymond Jungles, Laurie & Richard Stark, Dina Goldentayer, Black Coffee, Ray Rover, Ben & Natasha Gorham, Jamie Reuben, April McDaniel, David Bolno, Arlon Salazar, Francis Suarez, Icey Mike Imber, Stan Wawrinka, Bruno Soares, Loren Ridinger, Simon Huck, my late father Charles Grutman, Renee Grutman, Ian Grutman, Stephanie Grutman, Burt Grutman, Sylvia Finer, Mason Sharpe, Barry Sharpe, Candice Sharpe, Brian Sharpe, Nicola Siervo, Brian Gordon, Ryan Schinman, Rich Wilkerson Jr. & DawnCheré Wilkerson, Mikey, Sam, John, Daniel, Joseph, and Nancy Chetrit, Vanessa Hudgens, Mark Wahlberg, Serena Williams, Tom Brady, Rich Kleiman, Ivanka & Jared Kushner, Josh & Karlie Kushner, Anthony Rhoades, Aviv Nevo.